PASSPORT
INDIA

Passport To The World

Passport Argentina
Passport Brazil
Passport China
Passport France
Passport Germany
Passport Hong Kong
Passport Indonesia
Passport Israel
Passport Italy
Passport Japan
Passport Korea
Passport Mexico
Passport Philippines
Passport Russia
Passport Singapore
Passport South Africa
Passport Spain
Passport Taiwan
Passport Thailand
Passport United Kingdom
Passport USA
Passport Vietnam

PASSPORT
INDIA

Your Pocket Guide
to
Indian Business,
Customs & Etiquette

Manoj Joshi

Passport Series Editor: Barbara Szerlip

WORLD TRADE PRESS®
Professional Books for International Trade

World Trade Press
1505 Fifth Avenue
San Rafael, California 94901 USA
Tel: (415) 454-9934
Fax: (415) 453-7980
E-mail: WorldPress@aol.com

"Passport to the World" concept: Edward G. Hinkelman
Cover design: Peter Jones, Marge Wilhite
Illustrations: Tom Watson

Library of Congress Cataloging-in-Publication Data
Joshi, Manoj.
Passport India: your pocket guide to Indian business, customs & etiquette / Manoj Joshi.
p. cm. -- (Passport to the world)
Includes bibliographical references (p.)
ISBN 1-885073-23-2
1. Corporate culture -- India. 2. Business etiquette -- India. 3. Industrial management -- Social aspects -- India. 4. Negotiation in business -- India. 5. Intercultural communication -- India. I. Title. II. Series.
HD58. 7. J655 1996
390'. 00954 -- dc20
96-33489
CIP

Printed in the United States of America.

Table of Contents

INDIA

Waking Giant

India
Quick Look

Official name	Republic of India, Bharat
Land area	3,166,414 sq km
	(1,222,559 sq mi)
Capital & largest city	New Delhi and Bombay
Elevations	Highest – 8,000 m
	(28,000 ft)
	Lowest – Sea level
Population	913,000,000
Density	50 – 800 per sq km (130 – 2070 per sq mi)
Distribution	26% urban, 74% rural
Annual growth	2.7% urban, 1.7% rural
Official language	Hindi, English, 16 others
Major religions	Hinduism, Islam, Sikhism, Christianity, Jainism
Economy	
Financial year	April 1 to March 31
GDP	US$295 billion
	US$322 per capita
Foreign trade	Imports —US$36.9 billion
	Exports—US$32.8 billion
	Deficit—US$4.5 billion
Principal trade partners	Middle East, U.S., Japan, Germany, U.K.
Currency	1 Rupee (Rs) = 100 paisa
Exchange rate (12/96)	Rs 35.89 = US$1
Education and health	
Literacy (1995)	Women 38%, Men 65%
Universities	360
Physicians	1 for every 2522 people
Life expectancy (1995)	Women – 63, Men – 62
Infant mortality	70 per 1,000 live births
(Rate is higher in the north than the south)	

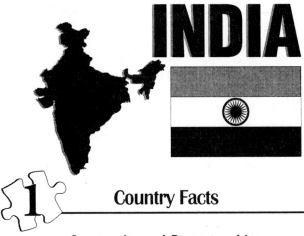

INDIA

Country Facts

Geography and Demographics

The Republic of India — Bharat in Hindi — stretches from a latitude just south of Japan to just seven degrees north of the equator. Set between the Middle East and East Asia, it juts out like an enormous foot into the Indian Ocean. Its vast alluvial plains are drained by three rivers — the Ganga (sacred to the Hindus), the Indus and the Brahamaputra.

Three thousand years before Christ, it was inhabited by Dravidians, whose civilization was equal to the splendors of ancient Mesopotamia and of Egypt. They were displaced by the Indo-Aryans, who were followed by Muslim sultans and kings (among others). Vasco da Gama introduced colonialism at the end of the 15th century. The Portuguese, Dutch, French and British fought for trade rights through much of the 16th century, with the British East India Company emerging supreme by the latter half of the 18th century. In 1859, following the crushing of the Great Mutiny, India was formally annexed as part of the British Empire.

This had been managed, in large measure, by the British East India Company, which first arrived in the 16th century to trade with the Moghul Empire and ended up owning most of the land by the 18th, including the nearby pearl-shaped island of Sri Lanka (Ceylon). After independence from the British was declared on August 15, 1947, the country was divided into India, now some 3,166,414 sq km (1,222,559 sq mi) and Pakistan. In 1971, the eastern wing of Pakistan became the independent nation-state of Bangladesh.

India is expected to become the most populated country of the world in the next couple of decades though, for the present, it ranks second for that honor after China. Its 930 million citizens are of a bewildering mix of ethnic, religious and linguistic groups who are further divided and subdivided by the prevalent caste system. In terms of average population density, its 267.69 persons per sq km is a little more than that of Germany. But India is a poor country, and it suffers from overcrowded cities and an infrastructure that's been overwhelmed by massive population growth during the last fifty years.

Climate

India's climate is extremely diverse. Parts of the Ladakh region in Kashmir are among the coldest inhabited places on earth; the Himalaya (literally, "abode of the snows") mountain ranges are also very cold (and remain uninhabited).

Temperatures in the northern plains and the western deserts can reach 49°C (120°F) between May and June, though their ground temperatures can be as low as -18°C (0°F) in winter. The lower peninsular India enjoys a moderate climate though it can get hot between March and June.

Monsoon winds are central to the life of the country. They bring rain and replenish the rivers, lakes and aquifers, thereby sustaining the agriculture on which most Indians depend for their livelihood. The main south-west monsoon brings rain between May and September (with Bombay and the west coast receiving rains in late May, and Delhi nearly a month later). The north-east monsoon brings rain to the southern state of Tamil Nadu.

Business Hours

Business hours vary. The central government, western-style corporations and businesses work between 9.30 A.M. and 5.30 P.M. five days week, with a one-hour lunch break between 1-2 P.M. Some state governments work between 10 A.M. to 5 P.M. with a half-hour lunch break at 1 P.M. Shops in big cities remain open till 7 P.M., but smaller family-owned businesses may be open till 10. Banks remain open from 10 A.M. to 2 P.M. weekdays, Saturdays until noon.

National Holidays

Some holidays are specific to regions, others to religions and national occasions. Various formulae are used by the government and businesses to keep them in check, but the results can be unpredictable. As dates for many Hindu and Muslim religious festivals depend on the lunar calendar, they can vary sharply from year to year.

The following are principal holidays:

New Year's Day . . . . January 1
> (Some states and businesses observe it, some don't.)
> India's urban population celebrates New Year's Eve as a
> "secular festival" with a gusto rivalling any in the world.

Makar Sankranti (in north) . . . . January 15
and Pongal (in south)   (approx.)
> Lunar New Year

Republic Day . . . . January 26
   Commemorates India's birth as an independent republic.
Holi . . . . March 5
   A spring festival in the north, it takes the form of a
   bacchanalia for the young.
Id-ul-Fitr . . . . February 21
   Marks the end of the holy month of Ramzan.
Mahavir Jayanti. . . . . April 1
   Birthday of Lord Mahavira, founder of Jainsim.
Good Friday . . . . April 5
Id-ul-Zuha . . . . April 29
   Goat killed as symbolic sacrifice of Abraham at end of
   pilgrimage to Mecca.
Buddha Purnima. . . . . May 5 (approx.)
   Birthday of Lord Buddha on the full moon day.
Muharram . . . . May 28
   Commemorates the martyrdom of the nephews of the
   Prophet Mohammed.
Id Milad-un-Nabi . . . . July 29
   Mohammed's birthday
Independence Day . . . . August 15
   From British rule
Mahatma Gandhi's Birthday . . . October 2
   India's founding father
Durga Puja/Ayudha Puja . . . . . October 20
   9th day of Dashera
Vijaya Dashmi. . . . . October 21
   10th day of Dashera, celebrates victory of Lord Rama
   over the demon Ravana (good over evil).
Diwali, Deepawali . . . . November 10
   Festival of Lights, commemorating the return of Lord
   Rama to Ayodhya.
Guru Nanak's Birthday . . . . November 25
                              (approx.)
   16th century preacher whose teachings formed basis of
   Sikhism.
Christmas . . . . December 25

2 The People of India

Language

India is home to eighteen official languages and as many dialects. Think of it as Europe stretching from Finland to Spain. Two-thirds of the languages are based on Sanskrit (literally "refined" or "perfected"), an ancient language which is to India what Latin is to Europe. And like Latin, it's only for ritual and scholarship. Dravidian languages flourish in the South.

Modern Indian states are divided on linguistic lines. Hindi is the major language spoken in several northern states, including Uttar Pradesh, Bihar, Madhya Pradesh and Rajasthan. Punjabi is spoken in Punjab, Bengali in West Bengal, Oriya in Orissa and Assamese in Assam. In Western India, there's Gujarati in Gujarat and Marathi in Maharashtra. All have distinct scripts and well-developed, flourishing literatures. Southern languages pre-date several of India's northern ones. Urdu derives its vocabulary from Hindi Arabic and Persian. Once widely used, it's now spoken mostly by India's Muslim minority and in neighboring Pakistan. In addition, there are hundreds of major and minor dialects. Most Indians are bi- or multi-lingual.

The Prevalence of English

Widely spoken, English is the language of higher governance, of the judiciary, the media, corporate activity and higher education. It's the language of choice of India's middle and upper classes, who are likely to study it from kindergarten through college. It's also the common tongue between India's linguistic groups; an Indian from Tamil Nadu or Kerala is likely to speak English when communicating with a Punjabi, for example. Mahatma Gandhi, the non-violence apostle who is called the Father of the Nation, often wrote in English, as did his disciple Jawaharlal Nehru, India's first prime minister. (Nehru's *Discovery of India* is considered a classic.) Today, Indo-Anglian writers like Salman Rushdie, R.K. Narayan, Anita Desai and Vikram Seth have garnered international recognition.

There exist, however, sharp variations in the regional accents of spoken English; some can be positively incomprehensible to the untrained ear, not unlike Britain's Cockney or what's spoken in America's Deep South. On top of this, Indians tend to speak very quickly, and in unfamiliar rhythms. English words of Hindi origin include: cot, loot, thug, chintz, bandanna, dungaree, pundit, coolie and juggernaut.

Religion

Religion pervades Indian life. It spills onto the street when Hindus visit temples, or Muslims offer prayers or they, the Sikhs and Christians hold parades to celebrate holy days. It resounds in shrines and holy spots — which can be as modest as a stone or the trunk of a tree. More uncomfortably, religion sometimes rules the very air, with loudspeakers blaring hymns or calling the faithful to prayer.

Hindus form the majority. Their religion dates back to the great Harappan city states (2400-1700 B.C.) and the Indo-Aryan civilization (circa 1500 B.C.). Though there are sacred texts, like the Vedas, Upanishads and the Bhagwad Gita, there is no one doctrine or creed that links all Hindus. Hinduism's emphasis, as India's philosopher-President S. Radhakrishnan once pointed out, is "experiential as distinct from the dogmatic or credal."

In the 5th and 6th centuries B.C., a philosophical churning led to the emergence of numerous sects, two of which became major religions — Jainism and Buddhism. The former was founded by Vardhamana Mahavira, the 24th in a line of enlightened *Trithankaras* (preachers) and flourished among traders in Gujarat, Rajasthan and Karnataka. Central to its tenets was the concept of *ahimsa* or non-violence toward all living creatures. Some strict observants wear masks so as not to kill germs by ingesting them.

But while Jainism remained confined to India, Buddhism, founded by Prince Siddartha (a.k.a. Gautama Buddha) spread to China, Korea, Japan and Southeast Asia. Like Jainism, it was a monastic order open to all castes and both sexes, and it stressed non-violence and non-theistic solutions to the riddle of human existence. Today, Buddhism is confined to the mountain regions of India bordering China, where it's known as Lamaism. It also has a small following among the erstwhile "untouchable" classes.

Though partition took away vast areas peopled by Muslims, India is still home to a substantial Muslim minority (some 12 percent) — by some reckonings, as many as in Pakistan or Bangladesh. Islam came to India via Arabian traders, as well as by way of invaders from Afghanistan and Central Asia. The bulk of India's Muslims are converts to Islam.

Christianity and Judaism arrived via trade-routes to the southern state of Kerala in 1 A.D. But while the former has flourished as the Syrian Christian denomination, the latter population has dwindled, as many Jews have emigrated to Israel. (India is said to be the only country with a proud record of never having persecuted Jews.)

Sikhism began as a reaction to Hinduism and Islam, but it evolved in the 17th century into a distinct religion. The Sikh faith emphasizes the teachings of the ten Gurus, whose message was incorporated as the scripture (or the Guru Granth Sahib), which is housed in a *gurudwara* (Sikh temple). It stresses a communitarian approach to life and the Oneness of God, who is both formless (Nirankar) and eternal (Akal). Sikh males wear beards and keep their long hair wrapped in turbans. Driven out of what is Pakistan in 1947, most Sikhs now reside in the Indian part of Punjab.

A History of Invasion

There's still debate about the origins of the previously mentioned Harappan civilization (2400-1700 B.C.). The Aryans began arriving about 1500 B.C. and gave the country its brahamanical culture and caste system.

Alexander the Great's arrival and conquests in 327 B.C. had little impact, but the Greek kingdoms headed by his generals left a Hellenic stamp on the culture. The conquerors who followed — the Sakas (Scythians) and Hunas (Huns) from Central Asia, Arabs, Turks, Mongols from the North and West and Ahoms from Burma — remained to become part of India's complex mosaic.

Only the British chose not to assimilate, though their tenure had a profound impact. Modern India's form of government, its laws and legal system, and the proliferation of English as a spoken language are enduring legacies of Anglo-Saxon rule.

A Pervasive Culture

India possesses a powerful and adaptable culture. During the first century after Christ, Hindu civilization spread (through example rather than direct conquest) to Burma, Thailand, Malaysia and Indonesia.

The island of Bali still retains its Hindu past. The ruins of Angkor Wat and Borobudur tell of the Hindu cultural influence on the great empires that built them. Other evidence of India's culture can be found in the prevalence of Sanskrit and Dravidian words in Bahasa Indonesia (Indonesia's official language; *bhasa* means "language" in Sanskrit) and in the history of the Ayutthya kingdom that established Thailand in the 15th century. Ayutthya (or Ayodhya) was the capital of India's revered god-king, Rama. Indeed, seven previous kings of the present Thai monarchy bore the name Rama.

During the same era, Buddhism (which originated in India) spread to Thailand, though the dominant Buddhism of present-day Burma and Thailand was to arrive two centuries later via Sri Lanka (Ceylon). The third Indian cultural wave was the spread of Islam which also seeped in to Southeast Asia. Buddhism was also India's great export to China and Japan. It was taken to China by the Indian monk, Bodhidharma, who established the first monastery in Loyang in 69 A.D.

Along with religious ideas, India exported music, art, sculpture (especially depictions of the Buddha), knowledge of astronomy and mathematics, fruits, flowers and spices. India's national epic, the *Mahabharata* — fifteen times longer than the Bible — is the longest poem ever written.

Family

The basic unit of existence is the family. More often than not, it incorporates several generations, with grandparents, their married and unmarried children and grandchildren living in the same house and sharing a common budget. (When an Indian says "He's my brother," he could be referring to a first or second cousin. In joint families, the terms "elder mother" and "younger father" are used instead of aunt or uncle.) This system is now under pressure as more and more Indians flock to the cities in search of jobs. Nevertheless, family bonds remain strong. Siblings try to live near each other and to meet frequently. Weddings, childbirth, festivals and funerals are occasions for these extended families to come together.

Extended family clans can be extremely large, observes British-born Indian author Pico Iyer, resembling "a banyan whose tendrils stretch in every direction and whose roots are cast halfway across the country." Extended and large, but no less familial. "Jaygopal's brother's sister-in-law's cousin," Iyer continues, "would be treated as a brother, worthy of the same affection, open to the same demands."

Caste

By and large, every person is expected to marry into the *jati* (community) he or she was born into and to follow a hereditary occupation. Almost all Indians, including, surprisingly enough, Muslims and Christians, see themselves as a member of one of some 4635 hereditary communities, each with its own language and sociological identity.

Among Hindus, these *jatis* can (but don't always) fall into one of four *varnas* (castes) — the highest being the brahamans (priests), the next the *kshatriyas* (warriors), the *vaisya* (traders) and the *sudra* (serfs and workers). Today, upper castes (the first three) comprise 17.6 percent of the population. Another 43.7 percent are lower caste Hindus living mainly in rural communities as farmers and cattle herders.

Though the implacable link between occupation and caste no longer exists, social intercourse between castes remains limited. By the 18th century, *brahamans* were already dominating such "secular" occupations as administrators, teachers and clerks, along with a newer subcaste, the *kayasthas* (scribes or clerical workers). In the 19th century, they took to English education. By the 20th, they'd formed the core of the middle class, along with the *bania* (a mildly derogatory term for members of the trading and business communities). Still, change is always occurring, with various *jatis* rising and falling in importance, depending on the current economic value of their hereditary occupations.

Though most modern Indians say they look down on the caste system, it still functions as a social support system. The Indian bureaucracy, for example, is riven by caste divisions, with *brahamans* helping their kin, *kayasthas* theirs, and so on. Political parties often choose candidates with an eye on the caste demographics in a particular community, in the hope of tapping into "vote banks" of fellow caste folk, who are expected to support their own. (Even criminal gangs often recruit members of their own group.)

The Erstwhile "Untouchables"

Approximately 15 percent of Hindus are members of some 134 *jatis* viewed as "impure" because of their (often hereditary) professions — such as tanning or dying leather, removing garbage and night-soil (human waste), catching rats, handling the dead and conducting cremations. The very touch of such a person was believed to pollute others. They're referred to as "scheduled" (because they're listed under a schedule in the Constitution) and as *harijans* (a term coined by Mahatma Gandhi meaning 'children of God'), but the politically correct term is *dalit*.

"Untouchability" was outlawed in 1950. India now has an extensive system of mandatory preferential quotas for placing members of these *jatis* in institutions of higher education, in government jobs and in Parliament.

Still, many *dalits* continue to suffer as their ancestors did (and intercaste marriage with a *dalit* remains almost unheard of). The dirtiest jobs are done by women and young girls — unclogging sewers and cleaning out pit toilets by hand, a labor that may earn them 10 *rupees* (30 cents) a month. This is particularly true in villages and small semi-urban towns where plumbing is non-existent (and where, unfortunately, the vast majority of the population lives). "The middle-class consumerism that, after five years of economic reforms, is beginning to hit parts of big cities like New Delhi and Bombay," wrote the *Wall Street Journal* in 1996, "amounts to little more in the Indian heartland than images from outer space."

How the Indians View Themselves

Indians view themselves as members of a religious group, a caste, a sub-caste and an ethnic or linguistic community, but principally as part of an extended family — within which relationships and identities are sharply defined. Thus, the duties of a woman's father and mother (her *nana* and *nani)* differ from those of her paternal relatives — her father's father (*dada*), father's mother (*dadi*), father's brother (*chacha*), and father's sister (*buwa*).

Brahamans and *kayasthas* think of themselves as

being specially endowed with intelligence, while
kshatriyas and *jat Sikhs* look down on trade and celebrate their martial traditions.

Hindus pride themselves in being friendly to all
cultures. While their cultural traditions celebrate
ahimsa (non-violent conduct), the reality is that Indians are no less or more violent than other peoples.

Indians also see themselves as part of a community that extends beyond caste and family lines.
Bombay-*wallah* (*wallah*=from) and Delhi-*wallah*, like
New Yorkers or Parisians, are creating identities
and communities that cut across linguistic, ethnic
and caste lines.

Attitudes Toward Other Cultures

In a culture divided into so many communities,
almost everyone is "other." On a surface level, each
of the 5000-odd communities finds something infe-
rior about the others — they're either "too dark" or
"smelly" or "craven" or they're "crooks." Still, co-
existence, not conflict, is the norm.

The British colonial experience, which dubbed
even the lowliest Englishman a *sahab* (big boss), has
inculcated an almost knee-jerk admiration for
things Western, and an envy for Western riches. But
as for Westerners themselves, the feeling is two-
fold. On the one hand, they're seen as arrogant,
selfish, lacking in family values and having loose
morals. On the other hand, they're believed to be
hard workers who play fair and judge others by
their merits, not just their backgrounds.

When it comes to non-Westerners, Indians pro-
fess indifference, ignorance and even a sense of
superiority. Upper caste Indians, in particular, have
an enormous sense of self-esteem and pride. This is
the result of the exclusivist nature of Hinduism:
One must be born a Hindu. There's no process for

conversion, except in some new-fangled cults.

Another pervasive attitude, dating back to the Indo-Aryan conquest of early India's indigenous peoples (and strengthened immeasurably by British rule) is color consciousness. A fair complexion is considered beautiful, the fairer the better. For this reason, Indians tend to look down on dark-skinned peoples. Muslims are seen as being "violent," while the more recent violence of, say, the Germans or the Japanese, is ignored.

Some of these prejudices have been tempered by education and experiences resulting from employment opportunities abroad.

How Others View the Indians

Faced with generating interest in India's 1996 general elections, a reporter for a prominent American financial daily described how a menagerie of elephants, camels, yaks and mules ferried ballot boxes to some of India's more remote locations and how, in some places, election officials and voters had to brave tigers and snakes. Though the number of people affected were few, the story made it to the front page. There are very, very few elephants or tigers. Indeed, special reserves and programs are trying desperately to save the habitat of these endangered animals.

Short-term visitors are often perturbed and repelled by the well-off Indian's indifference to the country's mass poverty. In 1968, India's Food Minister estimated that 35-40 percent of his country's children suffered permanent brain damage from protein deficiency by the time they reached school age. There's been little improvement in the situation since then. And half of the country's 200 million children don't even attend school.

National Identity and Pride

At the time of Independence, Indians were full of a great sense of national pride born out of their epic, and largely non-violent struggle led by Mahatma Gandhi. Not having seen the destruction of war, India was relatively well off, as ex-colonial countries go. But fifty years down the line — with its economy barely keeping pace, at a subsistence level, with a burgeoning population — India has seen one country after another overtake it in terms of economic development and quality of life.

To some degree, national identity goes against the grain in a country where people think of themselves as belonging to a *jati* first, and only then to an ethnic or linguistic group.

Still, entrepreneurs and industrialists have national business interests, and the middle classes pursue job opportunities across the nation or are part of the administrative service elite, which runs the state and local governments. These persons may still identify themselves by caste and linguistic origins, but in terms of taste, outlook and perceptions, they have a national perspective and, indeed, pride.

3   Cultural Stereotypes

Corrupt

Graft and bribery are endemic.

It's true that since the death of Gandhi and Nehru, India's bureaucracy has become riddled with greed. Low-level salaries and strict controls inaugurated by a political elite are two of several reasons why payoffs, tax evasion and "black" money have become a way of life. However, not everyone "plays the game." (For more on this, see Chapter 14).

Out of Touch

India has yet to enter the 20th century.

Though the culture is ancient, most Indians rush like lemmings into the sea of contemporary culture. Indian youth dress like their Western counterparts and listen to American popular music. About 50 million households have TV sets (more than Britain and France combined), and satellite channels offer everything from local broadcasts to CNN. The middle class may not have dishwashers, large refrigerators or two cars and a detached house, but most have live-in help for cooking, cleaning and childcare.

Environmental protection is now being given serious attention — air-pollution standards for major cities, mandatory lead-free gas for new cars, a Ganges River clean-up program, the closing of hundreds of polluting factories, and efforts to counteract the effects of acid rain (which, scientists say, could destroy the famed Taj Mahal in a mere fifty years).

India's industrial workforce manufactures everything from motor cars and giant rockets to telecommunications satellites and super computers, all of Indian design. And as many as 540 million people voted in the last election.

Superstitious

Indians are steeped in myth and magic.

Whether or not a prime minister takes office is determined by the President of the Republic, but the actual moment of oath-taking depends on the advice of astrologers. Like Hong Kong executives (who consult *feng shui* experts) or former U.S. First Lady Nancy Reagan (who kept tabs on her husband's astrological chart), many Indian businessmen and industrialists will not sign a deal, initiate discussions, or inaugurate a plant without ascertaining the most auspicious moment ahead of time.

Among India's semi-literate and illiterate, belief in magic, spells and incantation is all-pervasive. Talismans to ward off evil, chants to assist an enterprise and animal sacrifice to propitiate deities are common. Politicians and businessmen often wear rings mounted with precious and semi-precious stones that are believed to possess beneficial powers. Many of these same men are said to consult god-men (some reputedly practising dark Tantric rites) in order to gain "advance" information about future enterprises.

Almost every child, especially those of the elite

castes, has its horoscope cast at birth. Most Hindu marriages are arranged after ensuring that there's no major astrological incompatibility, and the ceremony almost always takes place in the "right" month and at the "right" hour. (See Chapter 17: Customs).

The mix of old and new can be seen in computer-controlled machines and lathes festooned with garlands and worshipped once a year — an update of the tradition of worshiping the implements of one's profession. Computers and taxi dashboards sometimes sport small pictures of a god or goddess and are marked with a dash of *vibhuti* (sacred ash). This doesn't reflect a belief that magical forces will keep the machines running, but rather, a deep faith in God.

Unhygienic

Indians are dirty and poor.

Mahatma Gandhi's promise of a future free of deprivation remains unfulfilled, if not forgotten, in hundreds of thousands of villages, where even safe drinking water and healthcare are lacking. The fact that the population has nearly tripled since Gandhi's day hasn't helped. One former prime minister estimates that 85 percent of all monies slated for the poor (the equivalent of billions of US dollars annually) is stolen by corrupt officials before it ever reaches them.

Most of India lacks what Westerners think of as plumbing. People use the fields for a toilet. Urban Indians are likely to bathe twice a day in hot weather, despite water shortages.

Unpleasant

Educated Indians are either arrogant or "oily."

Some Westerners are irritated by educated, well-read, self-confident, English-speaking Indians who refuse to conform to the stereotype of semi-literate Third Worlders who need "guidance" into the modern world.

Others see Indians as needlessly fawning. The caste system, augmented by a feudal/colonial history, has left a tradition of politeness that often borders on obsequiousness. In some instances, this behavior is nothing more than an irritating habit. In others, it's a way of extracting favors or concessions. Among poorer people and people of lower-caste origins, it tends to be servility, an unfortunate consequence of having been condemned to live, for generations, as an exploited underclass.

Maimed Children

Poor Indians maim their offspring in order to make them better beggars.

This is the kind of bogeyman story that often makes the rounds of media. While it's true that the poor and physically afflicted are often forced to beg for a living, their misfortunes aren't the result of such deliberate cruelty. It's also true that many beggars are skillful actors and make-up artists.

4 Regional Differences

North vs. South

The broadest divisions exist between the north and south, with the Vindhya mountain range serving as a natural dividing line. Northerners see southerners as being dark-complexioned, clever, and sometimes too clever by half. Southerners do tend to be a shade darker than their neighbors, but there are also dark-skinned northerners and fair southerners. Southerners, for their part, see northerners as brash, somewhat uncouth and violent.

Northerners eat *chapatis* (unleavened bread) while southerners eat rice. Traditionally, northern males wore *dhotis* (fabric that they pleat and tuck under the leg, then hitch at the back) and *paijamas* (pyjama-like trousers), while their southern counterparts wore only *dhotis*, which they wrap around like a long skirt. Married women in the north can be identified by the vermilion powder they daub on the center parting of their hair. Their counterparts wear a *mangalsutra*, a necklace made of gold and black beads.

Northerners pride themselves on their martial prowess, while southerners, no mean warriors when it comes to business, don't. In the Indian armed forces, northerners are known as technical whiz-kids who man the electronics, technical and engineering branches. Northern states like Punjab are renowned for agriculture and what's termed the "small-scale" industrial sector, which includes garments, sporting goods, electronics and automotive components.

Southern states have a concentration of heavy industry. Andhra Pradesh is known for shipbuilding, oil refining and steel, and Hyderabad for electronic, machine tool and aerospace industries. A massive aerospace complex can also be found in Bangalore, the premier center of India's burgeoning software industry. (Many strategic industries were established in the south because of the area's relative safety from air attack.)

Kerala is the most densely populated and most literate (90 percent) state, and its quality of life is considered India's highest. Nurses from Kerala are the backbone of not just India's but the Middle East's healthcare systems, and they can also be found working in Germany, the U.S. and Canada. Tamil Nadu, home to the city of Madras, has oil refineries and railway coach manufacturing facilities, in addition to a range of automotive, chemical, cement and fertilizer industries.

Neglected East vs. Entrepreneurial West

The eastern region consists of Bihar, West Bengal (whose capital is Calcutta), Orissa, and the 'Seven Sisters' — Assam, Arunachal, Meghalaya, Tripura, Mizoram, Manipur and Nagaland. The first three are populous and poor (though rich in minerals). Calcutta, once India's leading city, is seeking to reclaim that title via its heavy engineering and steel industries, and by adding petrochemicals, electronics and software to its repertoire. Until the 1960's, Calcutta was known as "the Shanghai of South Asia," due to its large Chinese population, some 20,000 strong. (Most slowly drifted away due to prejudice and lack of employment opportunities.)

Gujarat, Rajasthan and Maharashtra comprise the western states. Gujarat's port of Surat was where the British East India company established its first trading post. Today, Gujarat remains a major textile, cement, chemical, petrochemical and pharmaceutical center. Rajasthan is best known for its great forts and desert scenery. Maharashtra is India's premier industrial state. Oil, petrochemical, automotive and engineering industries are concentrated here, and software is also burgeoning.

Mumbai (Bombay)

The city came to the British as part of the 16th century dowry of a Portuguese princess. It wasn't much of a city then, more a malarial island with a small trading post, but it grew into a bustling industrial port and India's largest city.

Due to expansion limitations, the price of office space has increased as much as 500 percent since 1991, giving Mumbai the distinction of having real estate rates that top those in Tokyo or New York City. Antique red London buses and wooden lorries compete with Mercedes and BMWs. The city's air is so polluted that spending 24 hours there is said to be the equivalent of smoking a pack of cigarettes.

But despite its problems, Mumbai provides the largest share of India's direct taxes, channels nearly half its foreign trade, is headquarters for a number of top corporations, and home to a stock exchange that lists over 6,000 companies. The city has another side, too. It's home to the Parsis (Zoroastrians), an ancient fire-worshiping people who lay out their dead on the Towers of Silence as food for local vultures.

5 Government & Business

Self Reliance vs. Nationalization

Politics and business have always been bedfellows in India. The Congress Party, established 27 years after Britain annexed India, fought an ongoing battle for national self-rule, and a number of top Indian businessmen played important roles as advisers and quiet fund-raisers. Mahatma Gandhi, the Party's dominant leader, advocated peaceful non-cooperation (*satyagraha*) and the boycott of British goods. When the Mahatma (literally, "great soul") was assassinated during a prayer meeting in Delhi in 1948, it was in a businessman's home in which Gandhi had been a regular guest. (The house was subsequently donated to the nation and converted into a shrine.)

Gandhi had advocated self-reliance and the promotion of small and rural industries. After his death, Jawaharlal Nehru (India's first prime minister) endorsed an ambitious program of industrialization, central planning, and state ownership of core sectors of the country's steel, power, coal mining and transportation industries. Industrialists supported these ideas (known as the 'Bombay Plan') in the belief the burden of infrastructure development would fall on the government, leaving the lucrative fields of consumer and light engineering industries to them.

The License-Quota-Subsidy Raj

Established in the 1950s, the license-quota-subsidy *raj* (governance) allowed those who possessed a bit of paper signed by a bureaucrat or minister to raise investment capital or find a business partner. Many industrialists used their influence to ensure that no one could get a license that would allow them to create products that might threaten their monopoly. On top of this, import controls were introduced in 1957, in the wake of a foreign exchange crisis. Some imports were banned; others were restricted. All were subject to tariff.

Because government quotas restricted capacities and closed areas, companies were forced to look for profit in whatever business they could land a license for, or an import quota. Even a venerable company like Tatas, whose core competency was in steel, heavy engineering and automotives, ended up involved in tea gardening, oil and soap production.

Very tangible examples of this flawed system were the ubiquitous Ambassador and Premier cars, both manufactured from licenses obtained in the 1950s from the U.K. and Italy. Since cars were deemed luxuries, the government refused permission to anyone to modernize them. The Indian consumer was forced to accept whatever was offered. Indian entrepreneurs, often through "influence," obtained dirt-cheap licenses for obsolete consumer electronic products, then retailed them to a captive market at fantastic profits.

Since the state owned the power companies, distribution, railways, roads and ports, people assumed that it was their right to obtain these services at little or no cost. Union workers believed that the main purpose of these companies was to provide them with employment. To compound all this, the government nationalized all banks in 1969, having previously nationalized the insurance industry.

By the 1970s, the license-quota-subsidy *raj* had become a Frankenstein with a stranglehold over the country's economic progress. The industrialists' previous support waned when they realized that these rules and regulations, far from promoting socialistic or any other ideals, had helped to create a vast network of corruption and graft. Some of them worried that political rivals were manipulating tariff rates, license regulations and financing to their detriment.

The denouement occurred in the 1980s, when an "outsider" (a person with no fortune to back him) — Dirubhai Ambani — allegedly used the system to manipulate import duties and tariffs, issue duplicate shares, switch thousands of stock certificates to avoid capital-gains taxes, and buy up shares to bolster prices, thereby creating Reliance Industries (India's biggest and most widely held enterprise) within the space of fifteen years. Reliance, in turn, accused a "bear cartel" of hostile brokers of intentionally depressing Reliance shares and selling borrowed shares in the hope of replacing them at a lower price. (Ambani's company specializes in textiles and petrochemicals. As of late 1996, no final determination on the allegations has been made.)

Though the Raj had been implemented, to a large extent, in the name of the poor, it was the Indian middle and upper classes who benefited. University education was virtually free, reflecting a subsidy mainly to those who were already well-off, while vast pockets of rural illiteracy remained.

Metro-rail fares in Bombay and fertilizers were both subsidized, but neither were used by the poor. Likewise, parking was free or very inexpensive in most Indian cities, once again reflecting a subsidy for the well-to-do.

Why Politicians Are in the Game

India's politicians are aware of their failure to deliver the goods. The grand Congress Party, the one that brought about national independence, is in tatters, along with its "socialistic" policies. Their dream scenario was to change the way things are done without forfeiting the elections to other parties. The challenge is to formulate policies that both increase economic growth and ensure that the benefits of that growth trickle down to all strata of the population.

Trying for Change

Today, almost all major companies have the government of India as a major, if not dominant, shareholder via institutions such as the Life Insurance Corporation (state-owned), the Unit Trust of India, the Industrial Development Bank of India and the Industrial Credit and Investment Bank of India.

Current government policy is to disassociate itself from much business-related activity and instead focus on regulatory activity, poverty alleviation and social reform. However, past habits die hard, especially lucrative ones.

In any case, as of today, the top three companies in terms of sales still belong to the government. These are the Steel Authority of India Limited (SAIL), Bharat Petroleum and the State Bank of India (SBI).

6   The Work Environment

Generalizing about India's work environment is difficult. One reason is that a substantial number of companies are proprietorial firms whose methods are shaped by family members. Another is that the range of companies varies so sharply — from small sweat-shop-type garment or handicraft makers to MBA-staffed business conglomerates that manufacture everything from trucks to toothpaste.

A Beehive of Workers

While some modern offices in the private sector aren't very different from their counterparts in other countries, more traditional private sector offices employ a lot more people. This is also true of many public sector and government offices.

There are "personal secretaries" (PSs), who manage appointments and schedules. There are also deputy secretaries and joint secretaries. Beneath them are the *babus* ("personal assistants"), mostly male clerical workers who type letters and maintain files. At the lowest rung are cleaning personnel and the *chaprasis* (peons or tea boys). The latter fetch and carry files, get the tea and snacks, cash or deposit checks, pay telephone bills, pick up airline tickets, and so on. They often belong to impecunious, semi-literate, upper-caste families from rural areas.

The divisions are quite rigid (and familiarity between the ranks discouraged), though an ambitious person can move up if he or she can clear the requisite examinations. While female workers and executives are not uncommon, middle-rung personnel (such as shop-floor supervisors) tend to be male. While private sector careers are open to talent, caste prejudice continues to play a role.

Status in the Workplace

Indians are a status-conscious people, and this manifests in a number of ways. It's not uncommon to see a senior executive leaving the office with his *chaprasi* carrying his briefcase. A *babu* will not fetch tea for the boss, as that's the *chaprasi's* job.

In government, there's a Warrant of Precedence, which lays down the hierarchy in detail. Salaries are another measure of rank. Formally, the President of India gets a salary of Rs 10,0000 (US$280) per month, along with various allowances; a top-most civil servant may draw a basic pay of Rs 8,000. (Typical private sector salaries may be five to ten times that amount, plus allowances.) Of course, the president gets to stay in the Lutyens-designed Presidential Palace in New Delhi. Civil servants live in rental houses, in choice localities, for which they pay 10 percent of their salaries.

There's one important caveat. Because many firms are proprietorial, rank doesn't always designate true status. Family members may not have formal titles or positions, but they're above all the others, including the company's president, in the totem pole.

Seniority

Indian culture promotes deference for age and seniority, particularly in government. Date of birth, when one was promoted to a particular basic salary scale, and in some instances, even the time of the day one was hired, A.M. or P.M., can affect how seniority is gauged — and that in turn forms the basis of appointments and promotions.

In the corporate sector, with profit as the main incentive, seniority doesn't weigh as heavily, but it's still associated with experience. The colonial mind-set may allow an Indian to accept a younger person from the West as a boss, but accepting a younger Indian boss will be difficult.

Nepotism

Assisting members of one's extended family is considered a duty. Hiring or promoting caste brothers is seen as a means of building up lobbies within the work environment. The person assisted may be a third cousin's wife's brother or an aunt's son's brother-in-law. Be it the elite Indian Administrative Service or the police forces, establishing and taking advantage of such networks is viewed as the natural Indian way of doing things. While the business and corporate world is relatively free of *jati-vad* (caste-ism), bureaucracy and administration are strongly influenced by such informal career "support groups."

The Indian Work Ethic

Peasants, craftsmen and private sector employees work hard, and many don't hesitate to put in extra hours out of a sense of both self-esteem and duty. But this work ethic tends to disappear at the government level. Workers arrive late and leave early, and in between they follow the dictum: "Do tomorrow what you ought to do today."

In small villages & communities, participation in festivals and ceremonies is considered part of everyday life. Attending a relative's funeral, for example, is considered a duty. And, of course, the definition of "relative" is far more extensive than in the West. Seeking leave from work for such occasions is not considered shirking.

Decision Making: Often Behind the Scenes

In the hierarchical Indian system, committees don't really work. Indians aren't comfortable with an "upfront" style, and they distrust "smart aleck" juniors who roil the atmosphere of meetings with unsettling comments or criticism.

A lot of horsetrading and discussion goes on behind the scenes. It's not uncommon, for example, for the Congress Party's president to discuss contentious issues with individual members of the top Working Committee in private, and then to call a meeting at which a show of consensual decision is made. This tendency is strengthened by the fact that most businesses are privately owned and operated. Decisions regarding new commitments, especially those relating to equity, may be decided within a small family circle over dinner.

Some proprietors still treat their managers as *munshis* (clerks who, traditionally, were chosen more for their ability to ingratiate themselves to bosses than for their knowledge or skills). But the younger generation of managers, educated in private schools and top technology and management institutes, refuse to be treated with condescension. Fortunately for them, their skills are in great demand and this, more often than not, is what's transforming the culture. Accelerated economic growth is another contributing factor. As firms grow, the top brass of both proprietorial businesses and corporations are being compelled to delegate more and more authority to professional managers.

The Indian Administrative Service

In its day, the Indian Civil Service (ICS) constituted the "steel frame" that upheld the British Empire's presence and authority in India, and it was the preferred career choice of many a British middle-class youth. Members of the ICS were well-paid and many were scholars — like John Maynard Keynes (1883-1946), an economist whose monetary theories have influenced generations.

After Independence, the ICS was replaced by the Indian Administrative Service (IAS), the organization that runs the "license-quota *raj*." Within its ranks can be found a species of influential government manager unique to India.

As with the ICS, entry into the IAS is through a competitive exam. Typically, officers join up after a graduate or post-graduate degree. Such jobs are coveted, as they confer both power and prestige on middle-class Indians. As state control has expanded to include a gamut of economic activity, IAS officials (originally meant to be general district adminstrators) have become managers of State and Union (federal) government public sector corporations. In some cases, they have magisterial powers. They've even gone on to head top government companies like Air India and the Mahanagar Telephone Nigam (the government monopoly that runs telephone services).

More important, perhaps, is that virtually all decisions regarding licenses, proposals, exemptions and the like are made within the government administrative divisions they head. Some IAS members also serve in an ex-officio capacity on the Board of Directors of many top financial institutions, banks and public sector corporations.

Since the minimum qualification for the IAS is a bachelor's degree in liberal arts, many members lack the management education backgrounds their positions require. To compound this, seniority, rather than previous experience, is the key consideration when it comes to job appointments.

An earlier generation of IAS officials saw themselves as guardians of the public trust. But today, with a newer breed of official willing to do the bidding of corrupt ministers, honest officials are, more often than not, sequestered into out-of-the-way jobs. For better or worse (largely the latter), these are the people who run the government. In the opinion of many, they constitute the biggest obstacle to further liberalization, and they're not likely to give up their regime of rules and regulations, the source of their power and authority, without a fight.

Many professionals, engineers, doctors and managers in the public sector resent the IAS's intrusion into their sphere, but they're helpless to do anything about it. However, in recent years, with the opening of the economy and the relative decline of the government's influence over society, IAS jobs have become less attractive. The best and the brightest now follow careers abroad and in the corporate world, and they do so based on their education, skills and on-the-job experience.

7 Women in Business

No Suttee, But No Re-Marriage

Traditionally, Indian women were homemakers. Even the status of upper-caste women was completely dependent on their roles as wives, mothers and sisters.

The upper castes (especially in the north) were kept in *purdah* — in public, their heads and faces were covered with the end of their *saris* (the traditional one-piece garment), and in private, they were confined to special portions of the house where outsiders, especially males, were prohibited. Today, except in the northern countryside, *purdah* is no longer observed.

And widows are no longer required to perform *suttee* (literally, "virtuous woman"), throwing themselves on their husband's funeral pyres — a sacrifice that purportedly earns the couple 35 million years of bliss together in the afterlife. Still, widowhood is considered the end of "normal" life, as upper-caste Hindus frown on women re-marrying. (No such restriction applies to Hindu men, or to Muslims or Sikhs.) Widows without means are often forced to do menial work for their families or in-laws, or are cast away entirely, regardless of their age. (It's not unknown for an elderly woman to have been a widow since the age of seven or eight.) Some families insist that widows become vegetarians, as eating meat is believed to arouse sexual desire.

On the agricultural front, upper-caste men are seen as masters, so only they may actually plow the land, but women do virtually everything else. They sow (especially rice transplantation), tend and harvest fields, and seek out firewood and water, often walking miles to do so. Upon returning home, they prepare all family meals and clean up afterward, meanwhile bearing the babies and rearing them. Females (including children and pregnant women) often eat least and last, and receive less medical care than males.

Some women own and manage small businesses like grocery shops, but always with the help of male relatives. The *mandi* (central vegetable market) in every town boasts a significant number of female stall managers. Women craftpersons play an important role in the traditional weaving and dying industries.

Trends

Suffrage arrived with the Constitution of Independent India in 1950, but with female literacy holding steady at 38 percent, its value to the majority is questionable. Western-style feminism, viewed by many as emphasizing individualism and self-interest, isn't readily embraced in a culture based on family and community loyalties.

While the lot of peasant women remains unchanged, middle-class women are moving into every profession in the land, including government service, law, accountancy and management. (In the 1950s, school teaching was considered the only "proper" profession for middle-class, well-educated women.) Commercial airlines employ female crew members and in the 1990s, even India's armed forces opened up to them. Camellia Panjabi (hotel management) and Naina Lal (investment banking) are well known within their industries. Shobhna Bhartia, scion of the major branch of the Birla family, is an executive director of the family-owned *Hindustan Times*. Anu Aga is CEO of Thermax (India) Ltd.

Still, vast areas of middle and upper management remain all-male preserves, particularly in the engineering and heavy industries. And while, traditionally, women were protected from sexual harassment by conservative social mores, within India's business environments, such considerations no longer apply.

Strategies for Businesswomen

Western businesswomen should be careful to maintain some distance from their male Indian colleagues. At social events, Indian men cluster at one end of the room, downing one drink after another and talking shop, while Indian women gather at the other end, sipping soft-drinks, discussing school problems, exchanging gossips and the best bargains in town. Visiting businesswomen should make efforts to mix with both groups.

Women are advised to dress modestly, perhaps even more so than in their native countries. Short shirts and any other garments that could conceivably be interpreted as provocative are associated with "loose" and "available" women. On the positive side, foreign businesswomen may be treated with greater courtesy and consideration than they are at home.

GOVERNMENT
TRADE
RESTRICTIONS

8

The New Business Environment

India Joins the World

The shift toward opening the economy began in the early 1980s, but it took a near-default (of interest payments on foreign loans) and a fiscal crisis in 1991 to shock the country into taking steps to dismantle the license-quota-subsidy-*raj*, lower tariff barriers, and throw open its doors to foreign investment. These changes have yet to filter down to the *babu* in New Delhi or, for that matter, to company executives and managers. And while there seems to be political consensus on the need to "open up," bureaucrats and politicians are trying to hang on to reins of power that are no longer economically viable.

- All industry sectors (with the exception of insurance and railways) have been opened up to the private sector, including state-owned basic telephone services. A similar system is at work in the domestic civil aviation sector, where state-owned airlines compete with private operators.

- Import licensing restrictions on intermediate and capital goods have been removed, and tariffs in certain sectors have been reduced from

300 percent in 1991 to 50 percent in 1996. (The goal is to reach 25 percent by 1997.)

- The Indian *rupee* has become convertible in the current account. (That is, foreign investors can repatriate profits and dividends from their Indian companies in dollars, but they can't sell or convert fixed assets.)

- Foreign banks have been in India for 100 years, but the limitations and barriers established between 1950 and 1990 have started to ease.

- A Security & Exchanges Board of India (SEBI) has been set up to protect investors and enhance the transparency of stock market operations.

Works in Progress

Most Indian corporations realize that the only way to survive — better still, to thrive — is to build on "core competencies" and to enhance quality and productivity to world levels. Then, they can benefit from their main competitive edge: the low cost of manpower.

Having flourished in a protected seller's market, Indian industry is now demanding a "level playing field." Some breathing space will be required before India can compete one-on-one with international companies. All are savvy and ambitious, but many lack the size, capital, technology and managerial skills to produce world-class products, or the marketing expertise to sell them abroad.

Indian Stock Market: An Insider's Game

Ordinary Indians look down on the "speculative" nature of the stock market, and those who invest are seen negatively as "gamblers." Unscrupulous businessmen and brokers have not hesitated to bilk the unwary.

Since 1991, India has been trying, through reforms, to provide the market with the sophistication needed to play a role in the country's economic development. Some regulations still need to be loosened and, at the same time, some regulatory mechanisms need to be tightened up.

With 7500 listed companies and a market capitalization of US$150 billion, the twenty-two Indian stock exchanges are among the most extensive in the so-called Big Emerging Markets. The Bombay Stock Exchange, founded in 1875, lists 6000 of the 7500 companies.

Since 1991, 400 foreign institutional investors have been registered by the Security and Exchanges Board of India (SEBI). Investments have gone from a mere US$4 million in 1992-93 to US$500 million in one month alone (February 1996). U.S. investment during the last few years is more than double the amount invested over the preceding forty years.

But Indian markets are, in the words of Victor Menezies, Chief Financial Officer of Citicorp, "over-regulated and micromanaged, ironically without effective supervision." They're not a place for the faint of heart. Reliance Industries (see page 31) used the stock market to finance its meteoric rise, raising US$1 billion through 2.6 million shareholders. (Stockholder meetings took place in football stadiums.) Though efforts are being made to reform the system, the stock market remains an insider's game.

Business: An Ancient Tradition

According to an Anthropological Survey of India study, as many as 543 communities have reported having ancestors who were traditional businessmen. While caste-occupation links are fading, there's one area in which they still work. Prowess in trading and entrepreneurship seems to be a specialty within the Marwaris and Banias *jatis*. They've been moneylenders and traders since medieval times, and possibly even before.

The Marwaris, hailing from Rajasthan, first established themselves in Calcutta and Kanpur, and then expanded their influence across the country. Today, Marwari families like the Birlas, Bajajs, Dalmias, Bangurs, Goenkas, Khaitans and Singhanias dominate India's industry and commerce.

Among the major Bania-caste families (the term "Bania" is mildly derogatory if used for a big industrialist or trader) are the Gujarati Banias like Walchand Hirachands, the Sarabhais, Lalbhais and Ambanis; Punjabi Hindu Banias include Sri Rams and Thapars. In some cases, it is quite easy to identify Banias by their surnames, such as Gupta, Aggarwal, Jindal, Khandelwal and Maheshwari.

In southern India, their equivalents are the Chettys, but Tamil and Konkan Brahamans are also prominent. The Tatas and Godrejs are arguably the biggest industrial families of India. Zubin Mehta, the noted conductor, comes from this community, and, it's said, still retains his Indian passport.

Maharashtrian and Gujarati brahamans occupy a unique position in that their entrepreneurial instincts cut across caste lines. The legendary business skills of the Patels of Gujarat have taken them to enterprises in East Africa and to hotel and motel ownership in the United States. The most ancient business community is that of the Jains.

Muslim traders have been in India for a long time, particularly in the west and east coasts. Among the better known communities are those of the Bohra Muslims, members of the Ismaili sect.

Opportunities & Challenges

9

During the past forty years, within protected confines, India's industry has gained tremendous managerial and manufacturing expertise. Companies make everything from steel and steel products, trucks, automobiles, tires, brake-linings, aircraft and aircraft parts to glass, electronics, chemicals, pharmaceuticals, yarn and leather goods. They've trained cadres of executives and workers whose skills could be upgraded to world-class competency with very little investment.

This industrial base provides low-cost, high quality components and services, as well as a built-in market. Did you know that:

- By the year 2000, India will require 40 million telephone lines. In 1996, only about 8 million serve the entire country.

- India plans to double its electricity production within the next ten years.

- There's one car for every 700 people in India today, compared to one for every two persons in the U.S.

- India's food processing industry is particularly on the lookout for foreign investment as a means of both upgrading agriculture and creating rural-area jobs.

Diverse, Burgeoning Opportunities

In 1996, PepsiCo added US$75 million to its previous investment into snack food, beverage and agribusiness, and Coca Cola is investing US$800 million. E. Merck is in the process of shifting its fungicide production with a 100 percent buy-back provision to Hikal Chemicals in Bombay. Fanatome of France has a production base in Kerala for its global operations. Swissair has shifted its accounts offices to Bombay.

International Equity Partners (a Washington firm specializing in private equity placement in India) is using its India Direct Fund to capitalize on the inefficiencies of the Indian capital markets — where interest rates are high (15 to 20 percent) and IPO (Initial Public Offering) costs are steep.

Indian businesses also offer "solutions" for foreign companies. Robert McIntire, a senior executive and management consultant, hired Mukand Steel to make special cast hopper frames for several major US railway companies who were in a bind when the last U.S. plant that made them shut down. General Motors is purchasing radiator caps from Sundaram Fasteners, a blue-chip Indian company in Madras.

Information is the fastest-growing industrial segment. Now that India is opening up its telecom sector, most big players — Nokia, AT&T, Nynex, US West, Ericsson and others — are already into or are bidding for the cellular services and basic telephony market. Meanwhile, the sales prospects for hardware like printed circuit boards, resistors, capacitors, oscillographs, test equipment, Digital Signal Processing chips and DRAMs are good.

Areas with potential include bio-technology (cheap manpower), agro-industry, food processing (the Indian diet is based on seasonal fresh food with virtually no processing or packaging) and pharmaceuticals. And then there's the automotive sector. Just fifteen years ago, two models of cars were made here, both via licenses obtained in the 1950s. Today, Suzuki has the largest presence, as it got started a decade ago through a joint venture with the Government of India. But Mercedes Benz, GM, Honda, Daewoo, Peugeot, Fiat, Hyundai and BMW are making themselves known. And Ford Motor plans to build a US$800 million plant in Tamil Nadu state with an Indian partner.

India's computer and software industries earned over US$1.2 billion in 1995 and they're growing at a rate of 40 percent annually; in 1985, the industry barely existed. About half the revenues come from export, and the country is moving from churning out foreign designs to developing its own. (Infosys, for example, has created software for G.E., Oracle, Reebok and many others.) Companies like John Deere and Caterpillar use Satyam Computer Systems of Hyderabad to manage their data via satellite link-ups. The fact that nighttime in the U.S. is daytime in India is especially useful; the Indians set to work while the Americans sleep. India-based Motorola operations have achieved the industry's SEI Level 5 certification, the highest in the business; only one other Motorola facility, in the U.S., has earned it.

Persistent Challenges

The largest single hurdle that India must overcome is its inadequate infrastructure. Power, roads, telecommunications, ports and airports are major bottlenecks. With the government reluctant to touch the state-controlled monopolies, movement has been slow. But now, they have little choice but to institute reform and throw open these areas to private sector development.

Several barriers to trade and competition remain. Industrial licensing may have been removed, but the Companies Act continues to govern, among other things, takeovers, amalgamations and inter-corporate investments. Certain levels of foreign investment must be approved by the Foreign Investment Promotion Board (FIPB), which is supposed to provide a fast-track but ends up slowing things down.

No reform has been carried out to alter rules that industries say work against them in labor disputes, and government approval is needed before a company can "downsize" its workforce to reduce expenditures. Despite liberalized import regulations, a ban on importing consumer goods (toothpaste, soap, processed food, liquor, canned soups, electronic goods, plants, seeds and animals) remains. And ultra-nationalist politicians continue to decry the arrival of U.S. companies like Colgate, Coca Cola, McDonald's and Kentucky Fried Chicken as cultural imperialism.

Despite dramatic reductions, tariffs remain high, and it's unlikely that they'll reach the promised 25 percent average by 1997. The U.S. Trade Representative's 1996 report estimates that without the Rs 44 per kilogram tariff, U.S. producers *alone* could sell about US$100-$150 million worth of shelled almonds to India.

There's also a lack of intellectual property protection. Brand names are widely reproduced. While India claims it's committed to patent protection, the necessary domestic legislation failed to pass Parliament in 1995. India's 1995 copyright law meets international standards, but popular fiction, videos, records, tapes and software remain highly vulnerable to piracy. While the scale of the problem is nowhere near China's, implementation is left to individual states, which are often not very active in this area.

Insurance remains closed to competition, though the government has committed itself to remedying this. Restrictions limit the ability of foreign banks to open sub-branches, and operating ratios are based on the local capital of foreign branches, rather than on their global assets.

Another barrier is the so-called "inspector-raj," which allows minor bureaucrats to shut down businesses on (usually specious) grounds that they violate hygiene, public health or labor rules. What is irksome is not the rules, which match the best in the world, but their selective misuse against foreign competition. Kentucky Fried Chicken, which was shut down in New Delhi and Bangalore, is a case in point. Fortunately, India's courts came to the rescue.

Some foreign investors have been able to create opportunities out of challenges. Dupont Nylon, which is tied to the Thapar group, found it impossible to carry on its project in Goa because of environmentalists' resistance. So, it quietly scouted around and one day announced it was shifting to the state of Tamil Nadu.

Joint Venture or Go-it-Alone?

A lot depends on the nature of the business, equity, the location of the target market, and on corporate philosophies and goals. Whichever route you follow, be careful if relatives and family friends of your supplier, distributor, partner or senior executive come into the picture.

Companies seeking to maintain quality control, secrecy of technical know-how and all profits often prefer to go-it-alone (GIA). However, one such company, Citicorp's Information Technology (India)

Ltd., benefited from its parent company's long-standing presence in India. And because India is a complex market, the GIA approach can land you without friends when you need them. The Dabhol Power Company, owned by a consortium of American giants that includes Enron and General Electric, found that out when their power project near Mumbai got entangled in political controversy in 1995. After a year-long rollercoaster ride, the project is almost back on track. DPC has now taken the precaution of taking on an Indian partner.

Still, an Indian partner may not be enough of a buffer for all eventualities. CMS Energy of Michigan has not been able to get promised counter-guarantees from the government, despite four years of effort.

Firms with intellectual property rights worries may choose both GIA *and* joint venture routes. Microsoft has a joint venture with India's biggest software firm, Tata Consultancy Services, as well as an India-based 100 percent subsidiary. As one wary American chemical engineer (ironically of Indian origin) points out, "Indians are very clever. Before you know what's happening, they'll reverse-engineer your product."

J. M. Huber went it alone after two attempts to work with partners. Its first joint-venture partner was technically sound but naive about legal issues that tied him to a competitor. Another partner, affiliated with an influential Indian family, didn't go along with the 153-year-old American company's corporate philosophy regarding certain ethical matters.

India or China?

Several thoughtful analysts believe that, of the two countries, India currently represents a lower risk investment because:

- it has a history of cooperation with foreign firms
- it provides higher returns
- it has a more developed legal system
- it has a more developed financial sector
- it has an established entrepreneurial class that understands modern business concepts and ethics, and therefore provides greater opportunities for fruitful partnerships.
- much skilled manpower is available
- English is widely spoken

10 Strategies for Success

Indians are hospitable people who go out of their way to cultivate good relationships with Westerners. But it takes time to graduate to the status of a genuine friend. India's business community tends to be socially conservative, and its members like to ensure that potential friends fit their mold.

But be careful about "friendly" relationships. As one businessman put it: "Friendships are useful. They cement business. But at the core of the relationship, there must be a good business 'fit,' an agreement on what constitutes sound business practices and ethics."

The Go-Between

You'll be told that connections mean everything and that the only way to do business is through bribery or by using someone's third cousin's friend to do this or that work.

A trusted friend or associate is fine, but probably the best approach is to work with a professional. The Confederation of Indian Industries (CII) and the Federation of Indian Chambers of Commerce and Industries (FICCI) play the role of go-betweens, as do top banks like the State Bank of India, Ex-Im Bank, the Industrial Development Bank of India, Citicorp, ANZ, Standard & Chartered and investment houses like Jardine Fleming. American consulting firms like Ernst & Young subsidiaries and Cooper's and Lybrand have offices across the country. The US-India Business Council (with a membership of all top corporations functioning in India) works out of the U.S. Chamber of Commerce in Washington D.C. and has extensive expertise.

Choose A Partner With Care

When Ford Motor Company decided to go to India, they selected Mahindra & Mahindra for a partner, a blue chip company best known for producing the Willys Jeep. But M&M is also India's largest tractor maker, and this has provided it with a nationwide dealer and servicing network.

Expect a potential partner to contribute both top-calibre management and institutional depth — for a start. Equally important are "core competencies" and financial staying power, and, to a lesser extent, the partner's market share.

Because of cultural differences, management style and vision are also important considerations. Some Indian businessmen still look at industrial enterprise through traders' eyes: Go into a business, make a quick buck and leave. This approach encourages a disregard for quality and a tendency to underpay management.

Many companies seek Indian partners on a 49-51 or 50-50 basis as a means of securing a foothold in India, with the hope that they can take over later, eliminating the partner altogether or reducing their holdings to minor ones. Indian companies, on the other hand, see partnership as a means of gaining needed time, technology and expertise to become global players. It's necessary, therefore, for partnership goals to be clarified before any agreement is finalized, or before "hidden agendas" can derail things. This seems to be the case with the Tata-Mercedes Benz venture, which began with Mercedes as a junior partner in 1994 but now seems to be aborting because both parties want a majority stake.

10 Keys to Business Success

1. **Set up appointments before going.** Meet with a merchant banker or representative of one of India's financial institutions (like the Industrial Credit and Investment Corporation of India (ICICI) or the Industrial Development Bank of India). Consult a specialist lawyer who deals with joint ventures and collaborations. A meeting with someone in the government, either state or federal, may be needed in the beginning. Allow time for short-notice, off-the-cuff meetings.

    Also, try to meet with the commercial or economic staff of your local Indian Embassy or High Commission.

2. **Make connections in India.** Once in India, seek out people from your own embassy or consulates. Officers there are now geared to promote business, they're very well informed, and they have extensive contact and easy access to the top echelons of business, industry and government.

3. **Look beyond the first friendly face.** There's no dearth of people with connections. Always keep in mind that partner selection requires patience and good judgement.

4. **Do research on potential competitors.** Before Dun & Bradstreet signed up Satyam Computers in Secunderabad for a joint venture, they

spent two months in India checking out thirty other companies.

5. **Be patient.** Don't go with the mindset that you'll make a breakthrough or strike a deal during your first visit.

6. **Don't under-rate India's legal system.** It's strong, and it's based on a Western (British) model. When political one-upmanship shut down the previously mentioned Kentucky Fried Chicken outlet in New Delhi, a court order had it promptly reopened.

7. **Beware of "under the table" tactics.** Bribery and corruption aren't needed if you have a good product and some patience. There are many Indian businessmen, government officials and ministers who take pride in their honesty and integrity.

8. **Offer your best.** The market can be both lucrative and competitive, so offer your best technology. By the same measure, be wary of people offering deals that sound too good to be true. They probably are.

9. **Use Indian talent.** India has a lot of managerial talent. Don't assume that an expatriate Indian who works for you in your home country is your best choice. He may be as out of touch as you are. Non-resident Indian managers can stir up resentment among Indian staff, who may feel they're just as qualified and more experienced. Hire locally, preferably from competitors, and then train him or her to your needs.

10. **Be flexible about deadlines.** Things move at a different pace in India. Overestimate completion dates.

11

Time

A Seasonal Approach

Indians are arguably the least time-conscious people in the world. In Hindi, the word *kal* means both yesterday and tomorrow. While it doesn't justify, it certainly conveys the latitudes Indians often seem to take with punctuality and deadlines.

Call it philosophy or cosmology, but the average Indian believes that things will happen when they have to happen. No human agency can change that. Perhaps it's because the bulk of India's population lives in villages or were brought up in one. In the countryside, time is measured by seasons, not by calendar dates or wristwatches. And the ties between city workers and their village families remain strong. At festival times or for the marriages and funerals of relatives ("relatives" can be an extensive category), a worker is liable to take leave or just prolong a leave of absence.

Government employees don't feel any need to be punctual, and rules are such that they aren't punished for it. However, the Bombay worker remains a model of punctuality and discipline. In the monsoon season, when rain floods the roads and metro-railway tracks, hundreds of women can be seen wearing rubber footwear and carrying a change of clothes tucked under their arms. Upon reaching their offices, they quickly change clothes and footwear — now neat, clean and ever efficient.

God's Will

Time is sometimes "stolen" by unscheduled occurrences — processions blocking the road, a small quarrel that balloons into a *bandh* (general strike), visitors (especially friends and relatives) who show up without prior notice, the summons of a boss who will feel slighted if not immediately attended to, or various unforeseen problems of a business or personal nature.

A Ludhiana, Punjab businessman, whose company is renowned for making wool sweaters, told this story: In November 1984, in the wake of Indira Gandhi's assassination, there were horrific riots and two trucks carrying a shipment of his goods were burnt near Delhi. As a result, he failed to meet his deadline and a German retailer terminated his contract. "We did not argue, it was God's will. Who could have done anything at the time? But three years later, the retailer was back. What we gave him was costing him US\$4 to \$5 per piece more in Hong Kong...."

Appointments

"Dropping in" or calling in at short notice is a completely Indian way of doing business, but it's not an advisable approach for foreigners or visitors from out of the city. Though the corporate culture is normally methodical and punctual, it's difficult to generalize. Many firms are still proprietor-owned and therefore depend on the business culture standards of chairmen, CEOs and company principals.

The offices of government officials tend to be

disorganized, and appointments suffer accordingly. Visitors are advised to add or subtract thirty minutes or so to their schedules to compensate for this. Ministers and their bosses may summon meetings at a moment's notice, without regard to time overruns. Most senior bureaucrats work late and over week-ends to catch up.

Call in if you have a problem meeting a deadline. Indians are aware of the hazards of keeping schedules and can be quite accommodating, once they've decided to meet you.

Time Zones

There's only one time zone across the country, though India could do with at least two, considering that it extends across 30 degrees of longitude. This causes the sun to be up unconscionably early in eastern India. But some things are left well enough alone. In a country where things are already chaotic, the addition of time zones would only add to existent scheduling headaches.

Indian Standard Time is 5 1/2 hours ahead of Greenwich Mean Time. This often causes confusion for international businesspeople, especially when other countries switch to Saving Time and Daylight Saving Time during the winter and summer months.

12   Business Meetings

In the 1990s, Indian corporate culture cultivates an up-front style. Issues are laid out and discussed in sequence, with bluntness and skill. Discussions can be free-wheeling, but deference is still made to seniority, age and corporate hierarchy. Still, many proprietorial businessmen continue to honor the old-style, feudal approach, i.e. loyalty is more important than competence or qualifications. Their's is a style similar to a poker game in which the ability to bluff is prized.

Arranging the Meeting

Initial contact may be through a friend, consultant or agent. Contact must be planned, but don't be surprised at last-minute rescheduling or cancellations.

Notify your Indian counterparts in advance about the officers traveling with you and their functions. This will be more than a hint to the other side to have comparable personnel at the meeting.

Before your initial meeting, have a clear idea about what kind of relationship you're seeking (to license your technology, establish a 100 percent subsidiary, establish a joint venture), as well as its scale and quality. Keep in mind that your Indian counterparts are likely to have done their homework on you.

The First Meeting

No formal order or format applies. Initial meetings may occur between core staff, including Chief Operation Officers and their finance and legal aides.

India's business elite are quite Westernized. On the outside chance that your meetings, or the negotiations that follow, aren't conducted in English, a colleague or associate can be called upon to help. Indian businesses are quite comfortable with professional slide and audio-visual presentations. Courtesy and a restrained style are useful, even when "putting all of one's cards on the table." Figure out the hierarchy and always defer to age.

There's a class of small businessmen who may put themselves across as having far greater substance than they do, or who may promise to meet deadlines that cannot be met. If you insist on open and transparent dealings, things probably won't go wrong. Though they may have lower labor costs, they still have to deal with production costs, overhead and depreciation. The point is that there's no such thing as a "dream" deal. Weeding out people "on the make" should be an important goal of a first meeting.

Business cards are now the norm in corporate circles but not so much in government offices, unless the officials are running state-owned companies. The rule of thumb is that the higher the rank of the person you meet, the less the chances are that you'll be offered a business card in return. The unspoken message is: You asked for the meeting, so leave your card. You know how to get in touch with me.

Negotiating with the Indians

13

Lake Swimming vs. Ocean Swimming

For the last forty years, Indian businesses swam and flourished in a protected lake. They're now being asked to swim in the ocean and aren't entirely convinced that they have the stamina. But as they're not about to abandon what they've built up, they've moved quickly to understand this new business climate and are aggressively seeking capital, expertise, technology and partnerships.

Tactics

While there are no specifically "Indian" negotiating tactics, the following guidelines may be useful:

- Indian businessmen are tough, hardheaded negotiators. They're very focused, very ambitious, they listen well and have clear agendas. Figuring out what those agendas are is half the battle.

- Be thoroughly prepared. (Your Indian counterparts certainly will be.) Identify your negotiation issues and put them in hierarchical order.

However, don't get overly committed to the order.

- Threatening to take your business elsewhere is a useful ploy. Make it clear at the outset that you're considering several other firms — but only if, in fact, you are. It's very difficult to keep secrets in India.

- Don't be swayed by such superficialities as a polished English accent or elegant table manners. And don't confuse politeness with diffidence.

- Flattery is an ancient and well-practiced art; Indians can be very articulate and persuasive. You may be told things that you want to hear, only to find that you've "lost the shirt off your back."

- Gestures count. Carefully planned ones (inviting a CEO and his wife to dinner, providing a cake for the birthday of a main negotiator or a modest gift for the child of an executive you're working with) can promote good will.

- Openly questioning a senior's point of view isn't the Indian style. If a question needs to be broached, it should be done by an officer of comparable rank.

- Nothing is immutable. Just as divorce is rearing its head in Indian marriages, corporations are changing character. It's not unusual to encounter the reserved, closed-style decision-making process and the more open style within two branches of the same family-owned enterprise.

- Negotiations can be intense. Issues are laid out in sequence and discussed threadbare. If stuck, it may be useful to bring in a third party (an auditor, lawyer, or even a fellow businessman) who is acceptable to both sides to break the deadlock.

- Particularly contentious issues can be dealt with separately, between the two top negotiators, then presented to the group for finalization. Others can be taken up on the side by the respective specialists (say, financial officers and attorneys).

- Keep some "goodies" in reserve and give them up at strategic intervals. Present them as good-will gestures, not as concessions requiring return favor.

- Many Indian companies have a dominant pro-prietor or shareholder, so it's important to ensure that decisions about equity participa-tion, raising finances, market share and level of technology transfer have his or her approval. Otherwise, the deal you worked so hard on may end up being short-lived.

Contracts, Indian Style

There was a time when business was based on trust and goodwill and one's word was binding. Even today, many commission agents, moneylend-ers and traditional businesses operate on promises that wouldn't hold up in a court of law.

But the modern sector of the economy believes in detailed legal documentation. The Companies Act and the Partnership Act, both modeled on British law, regulate everything from the formation of a company, partnership or joint venture to their dissolution.

While most companies have their own legal divisions, business also functions on "reputation." Dubious practices or breaches of contract often lead to an informal black-listing. (However, there's still the problem of pinpointing what constitutes "sharp" practices — actions on the boundary between legal and illegal.)

14 Business Outside the Law

A Brief History of Corruption

Most of the men who came to rule India in 1947 were from humble backgrounds. Even those who were well-off, like Jawaharlal Nehru, India's first Prime Minister, were inspired by Gandhi's example to spurn worldly possessions and cultivate a simple life-style. But within a generation, corruption and graft became all-pervasive.

Corruption, like water, finds its own level. Some, to salve their conscience, took bribes and payoffs in the form of traditional gifts during festivals and the marriages of their children. Others preferred cash, jewelry, Cartier wristwatches or even expensive fountain pens. A number of politicians and officials took money for services rendered through relatives and frontmen, and not a few had secret bank accounts in Switzerland or the Cayman Islands.

After Independence, in an effort to eliminate the notion of officials as *sahabs*, salaries were allowed to decline in value. At the same time, an impecunious political elite took over the reins of government and, in the name of creating an egalitarian society, inaugurated a system that took control of virtually every element of the economy.

The new system lent itself to greed. Even today, businesses must obtain certain government permissions, licenses or clearances in order to establish themselves or to expand. While some politicians are content to take a cut in exchange for expediting things, others demand a stake in the business via relatives.

Bureaucrats, for their part, have played the role of scavengers, dining on the not-insubstantial leftovers. Initially, the British-trained bureaucracy made a stand, but they realized that the politician-as-minister was their master. Many good men decided to side-step the process by taking appointments where there were few opportunities and pressures for graft. Others succumbed. The latter discovered the mother lode of money that could be made by slowing down, hastening, blocking or facilitating the progress of files relating to particular licenses, quotas or proposals. Telecom workers routinely turn off lines until their payoffs arrive.

Traffic cops are known to take systematic payoffs so as not to report overloaded trucks.   The police have been accused of letting off murderers for a "consideration" and the judiciary, particularly its lower echelons, has been charged with abetting some of these practices. And yet, in the past decades, it's hard to recall any major politicians, businessmen or senior bureaucrats who've been convicted of taking or giving bribes — though many have been charged, including several prime ministers and their kin.

The Art of Tax Evasion

During the era of the license-quota-subsidy-*raj*, foreign investment was restricted, and within the country, expansion, establishment of plants, importation of raw materials, etc., were determined by *who* was willing to contribute *what* to "party funds" or who could deliver the votes. In addition, businesspeople were expected to pay off an increasingly large army of politicians, *babus*, policemen, inspectors and others.

But such large amounts of money couldn't be raised by businesses that paid the lawful tariffs and obeyed the prevailing tax regulations. A complex underground economy developed. Big business houses employed an army of accountants and lawyers to shield them from the tax/tariff net via tax breaks and tax shelters. India's tobacco giant, the India Tobacco Company, may owe the government over US$300 million in excise, but the case has been languishing in the courts for years.

Some companies create a "parallel" economy, with its own books and methods of exchange. For example: An artificial silk factory smuggles in yarn from abroad or buys it from a producer who, in order to evade excise taxes, hasn't declared his total production. The factory then churns out the material in excess and fails to declare *its* total production, again, to evade paying duties. After government excise inspectors are paid off, the material is sold to wholesalers who will fudge *their* books. Finally, the material is sold, perhaps in the form of *saris,* by myriad petty retailers who keep no books at all.

Black & White Money

In a similar manner, through processes of under/over-invoicing exports and imports, many industrialists and traders (as well as doctors, lawyers and small retailers) have salted away fortunes abroad. The amounts of this so-called "black" money are impossible to quantify. In real estate deals, two prices are cited — one "black" and the other "white." In most cases, a deal is struck with a mutually agreed upon proportion of each being used.

The tax authorities often organize elaborate raids on factories, homes and other premises to check the stocks of raw material and tally them with production, and to seize bank account books and "black" money (which, being "hot," can't be kept in banks). The Reserve Bank of India has directed all commercial banks to report the details of all cash deposits and withdrawals that exceed Rs 1 million (US$27,000).

Rebels, Bandits & Thugs

The Dacoits, a kind of mafia that prey on pilgrims and traders, have a legendary, Robin-Hood-like status. Some gangs have developed international links, mainly in the drug trade. Opium comes in from neighboring Burma, Nepal and Pakistan, is refined in Indian laboratories, and then is shipped abroad. Criminal gangs, often formed along caste lines, excel at robbery, extortion and smuggling. Many politicians have developed links with such persons, since they provide "muscle" for intimidating political rivals at election time.

But it's in India's premiere city that organized crime steps to the forefront. Bombay's underworld extends as far as Hong Kong, Thailand, Singapore and the Gulf Emirates. Bombay's Fort area is lined with shops displaying empty cartons for foreign consumer goods — hair dryers, cameras, perfume, watches, you name it. Strike a deal, and the friendly shopkeeper will go around the corner and fetch the actual stuff. It's said that if you pay the premium, you can get anything from refrigerators and washing machines to Nikon cameras and French perfumes, all illegally brought into the country.

The most lucrative operations center around gold, which holds, for Indians, a fascinating allure. (Crime syndicates purchase gold abroad with drug smuggling profits, "import" it in 'biscuits,' and then sell it to local jewelry makers.) Gangs are also involved with prostitution, busting labor unions, money laundering and within India's movie industry, where gangland high-interest money is sometimes the only capital available for such a high-risk industry.

Another major area of operations is real estate. Bombay's rent control laws forbid the eviction of tenants, but street toughs will do the job for a fee. In the 1990s, many have made fortunes by assisting developers to clear sites they wish to build on in a city whose office rental rates are higher than Manhattan's.

Such "sleeping with the Devil" tactics have, of course, attendant risks. It's said that involvement with gang affairs cost the industrialist Sunit Khatau and the managing director of East West Airline their lives. Both were killed by professional assassins on the streets of Bombay.

By and large, such activities remain in the underworld, but they do sometimes surface. The horrific anti-Muslim riots of 1992-1993 divided the gangs along communal lines. With the help of a neighboring country, Muslim gangsters set off a series of car-bombs in Bombay that killed 400 civilians in one day.

Graft and Corruption

In 1995, India was rocked by what has come to be known as The *Hawala* Scandal (hawala = a traditional monetary transaction). A meticulously kept diary of a New Delhi businessman revealed a web of bribes and kickbacks totally 650 million rupees (worth US$33 million at the time) to politicians and bureaucrats of every stripe over a four-year period. The businessman in question not only bribed officials, but also functioned as an intermediary for the bribes of others.

Some prominent European companies figured in his lists. The government (which controls the Central Bureau of Investigation responsible for federal cases) tried to block investigation, which is currently being carried out under the aegis of India's Supreme Court.

In yet another scam, a state-owned fertilizer company paid money to a Turkish company (better known for its travel agency services) for 200,000 tons of urea worth US$38 million. While the company paid the money — allegedly to relatives of the then-prime minister and to the Minister of Fertilizers — the urea never materialized. Here, again, India's Supreme Court was called upon to force a CBI investigation. But unfortunately, the CBI's record of successful convictions is woeful. In a similar case, officials are accused of having created nonexistent herds of farm animals and siphoning off hundreds of millions of dollars for their upkeep under a government husbandry program.

In August of 1996, when police raided the home of a former communications minister, they found so many *rupees* tumbling out of plastic bags, suitcases and bed linens that it took them almost two days to count it all. The money is believed to be kickbacks for telecom licenses.

Such scandals have inspired tortuous investigations that involve everything from foreign and off-shore bank accounts to global front companies. Many have involved alleged "defense purchases." Apparently, no sector has been left untouched.

Present Changes & Future Outlook

Some businesses refuse to be "in the game." Indeed, India's premiere industrial house of the Tatas has a reputation both for the quality of its products and for its non-involvement in political shenanigans.

American businessmen, faced with the Foreign Corrupt Practices Act back home, have little choice but to say "No!" to officials who expect under-the-table remuneration. The road, though rocky at times, can actually become smoother later. The American chemical giant J.M. Huber refused to pay for the issuance of an environmental protection board clearance for its plant. Huber officials went repeatedly to the local Pollution Control Board Office but the document, *for a clearance already granted*, was never available. Finally, they got the American Ambassador in India to intervene. "Now," says a Huber official, "we have no problems. Word is out that we won't pay. You compromise once and you're stuck with the leeches forever."

As the government gets out of the "control" business and its role in everyday life shrinks, hopefully so, too, will corruption. (During the first half of 1996, an unprecedented 26 politicians were indicted for bribery by India's Supreme Court, including seven cabinet ministers who were forced to resign.) But such changes will be a long time coming, even in light of the present liberalized economy. Said one Indian politician, quoted recently in *The Economist*, "A government that lives within its means lacks imagination."

15 Names & Greetings

Order of Names

Naming practices in India can be bewildering. Fortunately for foreigners, Western-style name order (given name, middle name, surname) is becoming increasingly popular. An important caveat is that in parts of the south, both men and unmarried women place their surname and/or their father's name first, with their given names at the end. Often, the former appears in the form of initials, as in H.D. Deve Gowda (the Indian prime minister from Karnataka). The *H* stands for Hardanahalli, his native village and *D* for his father's name, Doddegowda. Both in the south and in Maharashtra, a father's given name becomes his offspring's middle name.

Sharma and *Singh* are the most common surnames in northern India. The former is always a *brahaman*, the latter never. Then, it gets a little more complicated. All Sikhs take the name *Singh* as their surname or middle name, though other *Singh*'s belong to the upper *kshatriya* caste. In fact, surnames often indicate one's caste. *Rao* is a title in the north and a surname in Andhra Pradesh, but it's used only by brahamans or members of the kamma farming community.

Some people dispense with surnames that depict caste (such as Chandrashekhar, the former prime minister of India); others have begun using their father's given name as a surname. Thus, a well-known industrialist family uses Sriram as a surname, though it was actually the given name of the family's patriarch, Lala Sri Ram.

Traditionally, the suffix *Kumari* was used to indicate an unmarried woman and *Devi* a married one. Today, married women adopt their husband's surnames as their own.

Forms of Address

Like the traditional greeting *namaste*, the suffix *ji* (pronounced *gee*) is appropriate for both sexes, regardless of age, and for almost every occasion. Attach it to a given name or surname and you take care of everything, as in Michael-*ji*, Jane-*ji* or Jones-*ji*.

A more familiar (though still suitably humble) suffix is *sahab* (pronounced like Saab, the car). For example, "Smith *sahab* has been very kind to visit us." It can also be used along with a title, as in "Doctor-*sahab*," "Professor-*sahab*," "Minister-*sahab*" or "Engineer-*sahab*."

Elders (everyone, not just relatives) are almost never addressed by their given names alone. The English *Uncle* and *Aunty* have become popular, catch-all suffixes. A colleague's college-going son will always address his parent's friends as *Usha-Aunty* and *Vivek-Uncle*, never as simply Usha or Vivek. So popular are these titles that teenagers and young persons routinely address anyone over the age of thirty-five as *Uncle-ji* or *Aunty-ji* in the North and *Sir* (pronounced *saar*) in the south. And it's not uncommon to hear someone addressed as *Sir-ji*

Teachers are always addressed as *Sir* or *Ma'am*, and it's not uncommon for Indians to address their professors or grade school teachers in this manner for life.

In the corporate world, the American habit of using given names alone has become common, but it's best reserved for peers and people of equal seniority. It's safer to use *Mr.* Tata, *Dr.* Srinivasan or *Ms.* Gupta until asked to do so otherwise. For married women, *Mrs.* is fine.

When addressing government officials, the prefixes *Shri* and *Shrimati* are used instead of Mr. and Mrs. (*Su-shri* is the equivalent of Ms.) In the south, *Thiru* and *Thirumathi* are favored among senior government ministers and bureaucrats,

Greetings

The traditional Indian greeting *namaste* (also *naamaskar* or, in the south, *vannakam*) is uttered while holding the hands together, as if in prayer, under the chin, slightly nodding the head and looking down. However, in business meetings, a firm handshake is most appropriate. (Indeed, a Westernized executive will be somewhat baffled if a foreign colleague greets him with a *namaste*.) When expressing sincerity or when saying good-bye, both hands may be used for the clasp. There's one key caveat. Most Indian women are unlikely to follow suit. The simple rule of thumb is to wait for the woman to offer her hand in greeting. If she doesn't, respond with a polite half-bow and a simple "Hello."

Indians are not quite used to saying "Good morning!" "Good night!" or "Good-bye," though the younger generation is learning. Likewise, "Thanks" and "Thank you" aren't part of the Indian greeting system, though *Bahut Shukriya* (Lots of thanks) or *Dhan-ya-vad* (Thanks) are used formally. One reason for this is that the feelings they signify are contained in the tone of the language and in accompanying gestures. An especially humble *namaste*, for example, could pass for a "Thank you" or a "See you soon!" for "Good-bye."

Traditional greetings are very important. Hindus will often bend low, touch the feet of their interlocutor, and then touch their own head. This is related to caste, but mainly to one's family relationship and the age of the person in question. A son will touch his father or mother's feet or those of his uncles and elder brothers. In less traditional families, a simple *namaste* suffices.

Muslims greet each other with the Arabic *As Salaam Aleikum*. A Muslim may also use the secular *Aadab Arz* (I offer you my greeting) while raising his right hand, palm facing inward, to his forehead in a salute.

Embracing members of the opposite sex is considered unacceptable. However, members of the same sex may hold hands in public or embrace if they happen to be old friends meeting after a long time or on special occasions. They may also do so on religious occasions, like *Eid* or *Holi*, by first placing their neck and face on a friend's left shoulder, then his right, and then the left again, three times.

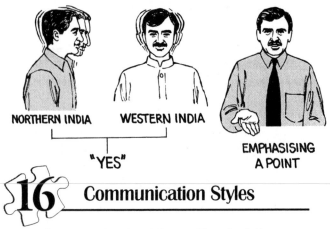

NORTHERN INDIA **WESTERN INDIA**

"YES"

EMPHASISING
A POINT

Gestures Derived from Classical Dance

For non-Indians, the most misunderstood Indian gesture is the northern habit of nodding one's head and shaking it from side to side. A Western engineer was baffled when, after an Indian supplier nodded energetically throughout their conversation, the suppler turned down the deal. "He said 'Okay.' What happened?" But in fact, the supplier was merely indicating "Yes, I understand what you're saying."

Indian classical dance has taken many commonplace Indian gestures and refined them into an art form. There are ones for every mood — anger, pain, happiness, and so on. The Buddha's classic gesture of the palm facing outward, with thumb and forefinger making an 'O' is the *abhaya mudra*, which signifies "Have no fear." At an Indian classical music concert, people sometimes shake their heads from side to side as an expression of deep enjoyment or ecstasy. At certain moments, they may loudly praise a particular movement by saying *Wah! Wah!*

So don't be surprised to see a lot of very different mobile gestures and expressions. By and large, no gesture is made with the "unclean" left hand (traditional used for personal hygiene), though Muslims may make a traditional prayerful gesture, with both elbows at their sides and palms facing upward.

Humor

Indian humor ranges from "sick" (handicapped persons can be the butt of jokes) to slapstick. Though people joke about other people's castes or religions, they're quick to take offense at jokes directed at themselves.

Western-style jokes, even somewhat risque ones, are fine if restricted to the company of one's peers. Wit and sarcasm are best avoided. India's version of "Polish jokes" are Sardarji jokes, told at the expense of Sikh males. It's well known that most of the jokes, self-deprecatory in nature, are made up by the easy-going Sikhs themselves.

Behavioral Guidelines

- Public displays of affection aren't encouraged. And deliberately touching someone you don't know very well, even as a friendly gesture, will only serve to make an Indian uncomfortable.
- Pointing is rude. A gentle signal with the right hand, palms facing upward, is polite when referring to a person or emphasizing a point.
- Indians may eat at street stalls, but you won't see any educated well-dressed persons eating in public, not even an apple or a piece of candy.
- While sitting, avoid touching those next to you with your feet. And take care not to drape your feet across each other, with your shoe pointing at anyone or your sole exposed to them.
- Indian's have a deep respect for books and learning. They dislike books to be left on the

floor or for books to be touched by someone's foot or shoe. It's not uncommon for an Indian to apologize for such oversights by touching the book and then his forehead.

- Indians are open and intensely curious about other people. Asking about salaries, marital status and age is considered friendly, rather than rude. You don't have to provide specific numbers, but do respond. If a question strikes you as too personal, the most gracious tactic is to smile evasively.

- When it comes to topics of conversation, politics is fine. As for religion, it's better to ask and listen than to comment.

- Be aware that some people can be "stuffy," especially in the presence of people they consider to be their juniors.

- As elsewhere in the world, "old money" family members rarely reveal the extent of their wealth. The "nouveau riche," on the other hand, can be uncomfortably flashy.

- Indians are used to foreigners and foreign ways, so don't hesitate to be politely firm on issues you feel strongly about. But do so in a manner that doesn't cause your interlocutor to "lose face" in front of juniors, peers or superiors.

- Like many Easterners, Indians don't like to say "no" outright. Sometimes, the lack of an answer is tantamount to a "no." In other instances, a "yes" without a follow-up can mean "no."

17 Customs

High Culture

India has a well developed classical music and dance tradition. Young Indians from middle-class families learn to play or sing Indian notes and scales and about compositions called *ragas*. They may learn to play traditional stringed instruments like the *sitar*, *sarod*, *veena*, or violin (played more like a viola), or wind instruments like the *bansuri* or the two-drum combination called the *tabla*. Indian girls are taught the Indian equivalent of ballet — the Bharat Natyam, Orissi, Manipuri, Kuchipudi and Kathak dances.

Classical music and dance are divided between the northern (Hindustani) and southern (Carnatic) traditions; both have their origins in devotional and religious music. Indian music has a much wider range of scales than traditional Western harmonics, and its scale notes are purer in terms of mathematical intervals. Another difference is that there's no pitch in Indian music, nor are there specific keys.

Popular or "Low" Culture

India's rich folk music and dance traditions

stem from the country's farming communities. Many are linked to births, weddings and secular celebrations such as harvests. But as people become more and more urbanized, folk music is transmogrifying from an integral part of community life into a "learned" tradition.

Cinema: Potboilers a Specialty

According to one estimate, India produces some 1,000 films annually, far outpacing both Hollywood and Hong Kong. The industry is sometimes referred to as "Bollywood," after Bombay. It has become a major cultural influence, a staple diet not only at home but throughout the Arab world, central Asia and Singapore. Bengali cinema, with its great directors Satyajit Ray and Ritwick Ghatak, has won critical acclaim around the world. Indian film stars are esteemed as cultural icons. Tamil leading man M.G. Ramachandran and Andhra superstar N.T. Rama Rao became Chief Ministers in the south, sweeping elections on the basis of their screen status.

In the early years, Indian films stressed historical and social themes. But the current trend is toward three-hour-long, soap-opera-like storylines featuring voluptuous (but saintly) women, nefarious villains, handsome heroes, lots of song-and-dance sequences and lush settings. Films that stray from this formula get dubbed "art" films and suffer at the box office.

Film soundtracks take advantage of everything from classical, folk and devotional music to Indian "pop" and disco played on Western instruments. Soundtrack albums are often best-sellers, and the industry thrives on repeat viewers — who often sing along, jeer, whistle or yell out warnings to actors about to be victimized on the screen.

Taboos

The importance of purity and pollution in brahamanical culture manifests as a series of cultural taboos, many of which pertain to food. Among them:

- The left hand is never used for eating, or for handing a person food or objects. This is because the left hand is reserved for personal hygiene. (Indians use water, never toilet paper.)

- While some Indians use cutlery, many prefer to eat in a more traditional manner — with their fingers. (The culture predates the invention of forks and spoons by thousands of years.)

- There's a strong taboo against eating and drinking from another's plate or using plates, spoons and glasses that have been used by someone else. An Indian would never offer someone a bite from an apple he or she has already bitten into.

- Many Indians are strict vegetarians and teetotalers, and strict Muslims abjure alcohol as well. Sikhs and Parsees follow religious injunctions against smoking.

- Hindus don't eat beef; cows have been considered sacred animals since about 700 B.C.; what passes for beef is actually water buffalo meat. And Muslims shun pork. (In October of 1996, McDonald's Corp. opened its first "beefless" restaurant in New Delhi. Featured is the "Maharaja Mac," a mutton-burger designed to appeal to both religious factions.)

- Leather shoes and footwear are forbidden in Hindu temples and in some homes. This practice is also observed by Sikhs.

  Seeing cattle roaming the streets and fending for their meals, foreigners sometimes find it hard to believe that they're considered sacred.

The average cow or bull receives no special treatment, except that they're not slaughtered for food.

Other Customs

To enumerate all of the country's customs would be a difficult task, but some are particularly striking.

* The *bindi* or dot on women's foreheads is not, as is often believed, a caste mark but simply an adornment.

* Some upper caste men wear a multi-thonged thread over their left shoulder, a symbol that they've participated in *upnayan*, an initiation rite into manhood. Once an elaborate affair, this thread ceremony has increasingly become an adjunct to the marriage ceremony.

* It's been said that the ingrained nature of sexism in Hindu society stems, in part, from the requirement that only a son who has gone through this thread ceremony (or if necessary, a nephew or other male relative) can light the funeral pyre of his parents. Cremation of the dead is the normal Hindu and Sikh practice, and it often takes place on the banks of a river.

(For more on customs, see the "North versus South" section in Chapter 4.)

Gift Giving

The giving of presents is linked to family and caste traditions. Thus, when a daughter marries, her female relatives may be presented with *saris*, her male relatives with cash. Gifts are also given to a mother on the birth of a child, during particular religious rites, and so on.

During the course of normal business meetings

and transactions, expensive gifts are not usually exchanged. Tokens are fine, though foreigners may wish to contact a local associate or knowledgeable friend on this. Top performing dealers or executives receive a variety of incentives. As cash bonuses invite taxes, paid holidays are a popular alternative. They can range in value and status from domestic destinations to proximate Singapore and Bangkok or to distant London and New York City.

The biggest gift-giving occasion is the Diwali (or Deepawali) festival. Gifts can range from a simple box of sweets (*burfi*, a kind of fudge, or Bengali sweets made of *chhena* cheese) to a hamper full of sweets, dried fruits and chocolates. A bottle of whisky is okay on Christmas Eve. All these should be delivered to the recipient's residence, rather than to his office.

When gifts are exchanged between a businessman and a government official, it's very important to be sensitive to the difference between what may be perceived as a bribe and what will be seen as a token of esteem or gratitude. The former might be a US$500 Mont Blanc fountain pen or a Longines wristwatch; the latter, a modest wall clock embellished with a company logo or a Diwali hamper. Not everyone appreciates the implication of overly expensive presents, and they may be politely returned. Well received business gifts include appointment books and customized calendars.

Marriage

Indian unions are largely "arranged" alliances negotiated between two sets of parents. First, there are strategic issues.

- Is the boy or girl of the right caste?
- From a "good'" family?

- Do they have compatible astrological charts?
- Does the potential groom have a good job?
- A good character and reputation?
- What assets — jewelry, cash, furniture, car, property, etc. — does the bride bring to the union?

(Dowry-giving was outlawed in the mid-1950s. In fact, technically, it's punishable by imprisonment, as it's come to be seen as tantamount to "selling" the bride. Still, many families pay steep ones in either cash or goods. Some businessmen pinch pennies all their lives in order to lavishly marry off their daughters.)

In the past, the couple had little say in the matter, and they often met only a few times, and never unchaperoned, before the wedding. And the marriage was expected to last "for life." (Betrothal at a very young age, now banned by law, is still practiced in some rural areas.)

The alliance is broached by an intermediary, usually a friend and relative of both families. Intermediaries also help to arrange an auspicious date for the marriage, to determine how much will be spent entertaining the groom's party (the bride's family foots the bill), the level of pomp and show that will be indulged in, and other details.

Indian marriages, even Muslim and Christian ones, are colorful boisterous occasions. In the north, the groom — on horseback, dressed like a prince — proceeds to his bride's house surrounded by a light-carrying entourage and a band playing hits from Hindi and 1960s Hollywood films. The ceremony, usually held at night, is a long religious affair that sometimes takes place in specially built tent-palaces straight out of the *Arabian Nights*. Though some families make an effort to keep down costs, others feel that civil ceremonies in dreary courthouses "don't feel like the real thing."

18   Dress & Appearance

Traditional Attire

Some members of the older generation favor a simple white *kurta* (a knee-length shirt) and a white *dhoti*, a six yard single piece of cloth tied around the waist — pleated and elegantly tucked between the legs in the North, or doubled and worn like a long skirt in the South (also called a *mundu*). And for headwear, a simple cap or turban.

A variation of this dress, found mainly in the North, is a *kurta,* worn with either loose or tight cotton *paijama* (trousers). Old-timers also wear a longish formal coat over this called a *sherwani* or *achkan* (cotton in summer, wool in winter).

But most upper and middle-class males wear traditional dress only on social occasions, such as marriages and parties; some even use the comfortable Indian dress as night-clothes. It's a pity, since well-tailored and starched whites, flowing *kurtas* and well-tied *dhotis* (see page 26) give a very elegant impression. Indian headgear seems to have fallen out of favor. The dashing turban is now worn only by Sikhs, who keep their long hair wound up inside them as part of their religious beliefs.

Peasants favor a simple *dhoti* and a simple garment on top, more like an undershirt. Some may not wear shoes and others favor tough hand-crafted *jootis*. The urban poor prefer Western-style trousers and shirts or a *paijama*. In winter, most simply drape a blanket or shawl over their clothes.

Indian women retain a preference for their traditional *saris*, one of the oldest forms of clothing. A five to six-meter length of cotton or silk is tucked into a half-slip, with one end draped over a blouse. They come in an enormous variety of designs and patterns and can cost anywhere from US$5 to $5000. They can be worn modestly, completely covering the wearer, or seductively, tight across the hips and low over the bosom. A poor woman may own two (one for wearing, one for washing), while a wealthy women may own as many as 2,000 of them.

In The Workplace

Indian CEOs often dress informally in summer (a neat, tie-less shirt, trousers and sandals). A hot-weather alternative is the "safari suit" popular with older British businessmen in the Far East. In part because offices and cars are more likely to be air conditioned than in the past, many younger executives and CEOs prefer Western-style business-suits and ties.

Working women, particularly in the northwest, lean toward loose, long shirts and trousers made of silk or cotton. It's actually a unisex garment, the trouser tied with a draw-string, but the male version is likely to be seen only in neighboring Pakistan.

19 Entertaining

Business negotiations will certainly feature meals, which can range from things brought in for a work meeting, to a business luncheon at a restaurant or five-star hotel. In some cases, there may be an evening of cocktails to which a cross-section of people ranging from government officials, media personalities to fellow businessmen may be invited.

For one-on-one meals at restaurants, the person who initiated the invitation pays the check. The custom of "going Dutch" (splitting the check) is considered impolite. Your Indian counterpart will always offer to pay, and he may be quite insistent. However, this is a kind of ritual, and if *you* invited *him*, you should pay. If you're of a much higher rank, insist on paying, regardless of who invited whom.

Dinner in an Indian Home

At some point, a visiting businessman or woman may be invited to an Indian home. Indian businessmen have large, well-appointed houses with a lot of live-in help. The food can be excellent, elaborate, and of a type never to be found in even the best restaurants — including fish, mutton, goat, chicken, curried vegetables, lentils, and rice spiced with saffron, cumin or cinnamon. But be aware that many business people are vegetarians, and many others are averse to serving alcohol at home. If you're particular, make an inquiry in advance with some other invitee, but not the host.

Expect to find anywhere from fifty people to a dozen or so couples to four or six people. A buffet-style arrangement is common, though more sophisticated, Westernized businessmen may provide a sit-down affair. Glamorous get-togethers often include live music. You're free to bring along a friend, but check in advance in case it's a sit-down affair.

A non-business dinner party will run as follows: First, a prolonged bout of drinking during which whisky (mainly) flows like water and prodigious amount of snacks and nuts are passed around. There may be musical entertainment. But by and large, drinking continues until 10:30 or 11 P.M., when food is served, followed by dessert — ice cream, *khir* (rosewater-scented rice pudding), mangoes and other fruit — and possibly coffee and tea. People begin leaving soon after, and postprandial conversation tends to be desultory.

Indian women sometimes refrain from alcoholic beverages and smoking cigarettes at such events, preferring to indulge in their own homes and among good friends. (However, there are no hard and fast rules.) The decibel level of conversation will probably rise steadily and a degree of boisterousness will creep in as alcohol begins to loosen tongues. However, it's rare to see a hard-headed businessman in his cups, even if he's drinking quite heavily.

20 Socializing

Indian cities offer little in the way of night life compared to, say, Hong Kong or Tokyo. India may be the land of the *Kama Sutra*, but its present-day mores are strait-laced and Victorian. So don't expect to see a local businessman letting off steam in a bar or out fraternizing with young women. He'll probably be home with the wife watching the latest Bombay movie on video. Younger Indian executives favor discotheques (often found in five-star hotels) and bars with loud music and Western-style dancing.

Bombay sometimes offers English-language theatre or concerts by foreign performers. Classical Indian music and dance are mainly winter events. If you're lucky, you may witness one in the home of some industrialist who patronizes the arts. The metropolitan cities often have art exhibitions displaying the work of Indian artists. Virtually any place in India is teeming with historical artifacts and sites.

Male and female colleagues may collaborate in the workplace, but they won't interact socially, regardless of their marital status. Dating, in the Western sense, hasn't quite arrived, though a slower, more genteel style of courtship (no hand-holding at first, no pre-marital sex) is not unwelcome to Indian women professionals.

Golf

This game has acquired the status of a modern religion among India's social and bureaucratic elite. Most cities have several good clubs. Golf courses are great places to meet the rich and powerful. Much business is conducted here, and many knotty problems can be resolved through relationships built up on fairways and greens. Foreigners can apply for a temporary membership or play as the guest of an Indian member.

Private Clubs

In British times, businessmen were looked down on as "traders" and kept out of clubs reserved for British officials, Indian landed gentry and princes. So businessmen set up their own clubs in which to gamble, drink, gossip and talk shop. Today, however, only businessmen have the kind of money that can keep such clubs afloat.

"Breeding, social status and the snobbery of a by-gone age still hold sway at these flourishing Raj-era institutions," observes the *Far Eastern Economic Review*. Bombay's Breach Candy Swimming Club (founded 1875) boasts a pool in the shape of British India. The Willingdon (1917) features 60 acres of gazebos, gardens, tennis and squash courts and a golf course. Membership in the Royal Western India Turf Club, as well as in the Bangalore, Tolly-gunje and Gymkhana Clubs are also prized. Many of these elite oasises are open only to the sons and unmarried daughters of existing members.

21 Basic Hindi Phrases

English	Hindi
Yes No	*Han* *Nahin* or *Na*
Hello Hello (telephone)	*Hello* *Namaste*
Good-bye	*Namaste*
Please	*Krip-ya*
Thank you	*Dhyanya-vad* or *Shukiya*

Many Indians speak excellent English, but Indian English can incorporate a variety of accents and word usages (some British) that can be confounding. As for the accents, watch out. For every Indian language, there's an English accent peculiar to it. Levels of education play a role, with the self-taught being the most difficult to comprehend.

22 Correspondence

A typical mailing address follows:

Mr. (or Shri) B.D. Singh
Managing Director, International Steels
21/C Ranjan Towers
Mumbai - 560-012
Maharashtra
India

Mumbai is Bombay's new name, and the number next to it is the Postal Information Number (PIN), the equivalent of a zip code in the U.S. or a postal code elsewhere. Maharashtra is the name of the state in which Mumbai is located.

It's been reported that mail addressed to Bombay is sometimes returned to the sender, as Bombay is now seen as a colonial (that is, politically incorrect) name.

23 ~ Useful Numbers

India country code .... [91]
International access code 00
City Codes
    Mumbai (Bombay) .... (22)
    Delhi .... (11)
    Calcutta............................ (33)
    Madras .... (44)
    Pune............................... (212)
    Bangalore .... (80)
    Hyderabad .... (842)
Police................................ 100
Fire.................................. 101
Ambulance............................ 102
Telephone assistance................. 197; 199
World Trade Center, Mumbai .... (22) 2184434

 24 Books & Internet Addresses

The Politics of India Since Independence, by Paul R. Brass. Cambridge University Press, New York, 1992.

A New History of India, by Stanley Wolpert. Oxford University Press, New York, 1989.

The Indian Epics Retold, by R.K. Narayan. Penguin Books, New Delhi, 1995.

The Discovery of India, by Jawaharlal Nehru. Oxford University Press, New Delhi, 1993.

Video Night in Kathmandu, by Pico Iyer. Knopf, New York, 1988. Offers a fascinating, behind-the-scenes look at India's film industry.

Internet Addresses

Economic Times (the main economic daily from Delhi, Bombay, Calcutta and Madras)

www.economic times.com

Financial Express and Indian Express dailies
www.express.indiaworld.com

The Hindu (major daily)

www.indiaserver.com

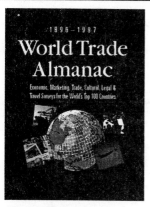